World's Great Scientists

Published by :
Lotus Press Publishers & Distributors

World's Great Scientists

Sneha Gupta

Lotus PRESS

4735/22, Prakash Deep Building
Ansari Road, Darya Ganj,
New Delhi - 110002

Lotus Press : Publishers & Distributors
Unit No. 220, 2nd Floor, 4735/22, Prakash Deep Building,
Ansari Road, Darya Ganj, New Delhi- 110002
Ph.: 41325510, 98118-38000
• E-mail : lotuspress1984@gmail.com
www.lotuspress.co.in

World's Great Scientists

ISBN: 978-81-8382-215-2

Printed & Published by : **Lotus Press Publisher & Distributors,** New Delhi-02

Preface

Scientists have made enormous contributions in the advancement of human civilisation. Throughout the history of the world, many scientists dedicated their lives for research and innovation. Some of them even faced a lot of torture for their theories but they continued their mission and thus we are now in a modren world.

Scientific genius is no easier to pinpoint than artistic genius. It derives from a combination of factors, including-but not limited to-intuition, imagination, far-reaching vision, exceptional native gifts that blossom into significant technical skills, and the willingness and ability to challenge conventional wisdom. Perhaps even more importantly, scientific genius depends on an instinct for invention, an ability to focus on the problem at hand, and a determination to pursue that problem to a successful conclusion.

This book attempts to present the achievement of some of the great world-renowned scientists who have contributed so much to science and the advancement of humankind. They have been listed alphabetically.

Author

Contents

1

Andre-Marie Ampere

(1775-1836)

Andre-Marie Ampere was a French physicist, natural philosopher and mathematician, best known for his important contributions to the study of electrodynamics. He invented the astatic needle, a critical component of the modern astatis galvanometer, and was the first to demonstrate that a magnetic field is generated when two parallel wires are charged with electricity. He is generally credited as one of the first to discover electromagnetism.

Andre-Marie Ampere was born on 20 January 1775 in Lyon, France. As a child he spent a great deal of time reading books on history, geography, literature, philosophy and the natural sciences. His father taught him Latin and encouraged him to pursue his passion for mathematics.

Even without any formal education Ampere began a career as a science teacher. After teaching for a while in Lyon he accepted positions at the College of France and the Polytechnic School at Paris, as a professor of mathematics. It was here that he first conducted important research and experiments into the nature of electrical and magnetic forces.

In 1802 he was appointed professor of physics and chemistry at Bourg École Centrale.

After a year in Bourg, Ampere moved closer to Poleymieux being appointed to a mathematics position at the Lycée in Lyon on Delambre's recommendation. Mathematically he continued to produce good work, this time an interesting treatise on analytic geometry.

In 1803, Ampere decided to leave Lyon for Paris. By this time he had a fair reputation as both a teacher of mathematics and as a research mathematician. Appointed professor of mathematics at the École Polytechnique in 1809 he held posts there until 1828.

He was appointed to a chair at Université de France in 1826 which he held until his death. In Paris he worked on a wide variety of topics. In mathematics he worked on partial differential equations, producing a classification which he presented to the Institute in 1814.

Ampere was also making significant contributions to chemistry. In 1811 he suggested that an anhydrous acid prepared two years earlier was a compound of hydrogen with an unknown element, analogous to chlorine, for which he suggested the name fluorine. He produced a classification of elements in 1816.

Ampere also worked on the theory of light, publishing on refraction of light in 1815. In the early 1820s, he attempted to give a combined theory of electricity and magnetism. He formulated a circuit force law and treated magnetism by postulating small closed circuits inside the magnetised substance. It is worth commenting on how quickly he produced this theory, the inspiration striking him immediately after he heard of Orsted's experimental results.

Ampere demonstrated various magnetic / electrical effects to the Academy over the next weeks. He discovered electrodynamical forces between linear wires before the end of September. He wrote up the work he had described to the Academy with remarkable speed and it was published in the *Annales de Chimie et de Physique.*

Ampere's most important publication on electricity and magnetism was also published in 1826. It is called *Memoir on the Mathematical Theory of Electrodynamic Phenomena, Uniquely Deduced from Experience,* and contains a mathematical derivation of the electrodynamic force law, and describes four experiments. The theoretical foundation presented in this publication. It helped to inspire research and discoveries by scientists including Faraday, Weber, Thomson, and Maxwell.

The ampere – the unit for measuring electric current – was named in honour of Ampere.

Ampere died June 10, 1836 in Marseilles, France, and was buried in the Montmartre Cemetery in Paris.

◆◆◆

2

Archimedes

(c 287 B.C. - 212 B.C.)

Archimedes of Syracuse was an ancient Greek mathematician, physicist, engineer, astronomer and an inventor. Archimedes, who combined a genius for mathematics with a physical insight, must rank with Newton, who lived nearly two thousand years later, as one of the founders of mathematical physics.

Although little is known about his life, Archimedes is regarded as one of the most important scientists in classical antiquity. In addition to making important discoveries in the field of mathematics and geometry, he is credited with producing machines that were well ahead of their time.

Archimedes was born in c. 287 BC in the seaport city of Syracuse, Sicily.

Archimedes is believed to have spent part of his youth being educated in Alexandria, Egypt, where he was a contemporary of Conon of Samos and Eratosthenes. Some of Archimedes' & mathematical works were written in the form of letters to Eratosthenes, who was the chief librarian in Alexandria.

His interest in mechanics deeply influenced his mathematical thinking. Not only did he write works on theoretical mechanics and hydrostatics, but his treatise *Method Concerning Mechanical Theorems* shows that he used mechanical reasoning as a heuristic device for the discovery of new mathematical theorems.

He was best known for his discovery of the relation between the surface and volume of a sphere and its circumscribing cylinder, for his formulation of a hydrostatic principle, Archimedes's principle and for inventing the Archimedes screw (a device for raising water).

The Archimedes Principal states: an object immersed in a fluid experiences a buoyant force that is equal in magnitude to the force of gravity on the displaced fluid.

He also invented things such as the hydraulic screw -(for raising water from a lower to a higher level), catapult, the lever, the compound pulley and the burning mirror.

In mechanics Archimedes discovered fundamental theorems concerning the centre of gravity of plane figures and solids.

Archimedes also made important contributions in the field of mathematics. He approximated the area of circles (and the value of ¼) by summing the areas of inscribed and circumscribed rectangles, and generalised this 'method of exhaustion', by taking smaller and smaller rectangular areas and summing them, to find the areas and even volumes of several other shapes. This anticipated the results of the calculus of Newton and Leibniz by almost 2000 years!

Some of his mathematical proofs involve the use of infinitesimals in a way that is similar to modern integral calculus. By assuming a proposition to be true and showing that this would lead to a contradiction, Archimedes was able to give answers to problems to an arbitrary degree of accuracy, while specifying the limits within which the answer lay.

He found the area and tangents to the curve traced by a point moving with uniform speed along a straight line which is revolving with uniform angular speed about a fixed point. This curve, is now called the 'spiral of Archimedes'.

Archimedes requested that his tombstone be decorated with a sphere contained in the smallest possible cylinder and inscribed with the ratio of the cylinder's volume to that of the sphere. Archimedes considered the discovery of this ratio as the greatest of all his accomplishments.

◆◆◆

3

Aristotle

(384 B.C. - 322 B.C.)

Aristotle was a Great philosopher and teacher who had a vast knowledge in different disciplines. As a scientist he made a good contribution which was very influential for the development of the science over the year.

Aristotle was born in Stagira in north Greece in 384 BC. He was trained first in medicine, and then in 367 he was sent to Athens to study philosophy with Plato. He stayed at Plato's Academy until about 347. Though a brilliant pupil, he opposed some of Plato's teachings, and when Plato died, Aristotle was not appointed head of the Academy.

Aristotle is said to have written 150 philosophical treatises. The 30 that survive touch on an enormous range of philosophical problems, from biology and physics to morals to aesthetics to politics. Many, however, are thought to be 'lecture notes' instead of complete, polished treatises, and a few may not be the work of Aristotle but of members of his school.

Though Aristotle's work in zoology was not without errors, it was the grandest biological synthesis of the time, and remained the ultimate authority for many centuries after his death. His observations on the anatomy of octopus, cuttlefish, crustaceans, and many other marine invertebrates are remarkably accurate, and could only have been made from first-hand experience with dissection.

Aristotle's classification of animals grouped together animals with similar characters into genera and then distinguished the species within the genera.

Aristotle's thoughts on earth sciences can be found in his treatise *Meteorology* — the word today means the study of weather, but Aristotle used the word in a much broader sense. Here he discussed the nature of the earth and the oceans. He worked out the hydrologic cycle. He discussed winds, earthquakes (which he thought were caused by underground winds), thunder, lightning, rainbows, and meteors, comets and the Milky Way (which he thought were atmospheric phenomena). His model of Earth history contains some remarkably modern-sounding ideas.

Where Aristotle differed most sharply from medieval and modern thinkers was in his belief that the universe had never had a beginning and would never end; it was eternal. Change, to Aristotle, was cyclical: water, for instance, might evaporate from the sea and rain down again, and rivers might come into existence and then perish, but overall conditions would never change.

In the later Middle Ages, Aristotle's work was rediscovered and enthusiastically adopted by medieval scholars. Many accepted every word of his writings — or at least every word that did not contradict the Bible — as eternal truth. Fused and reconciled with Christian doctrine into a philosophical system known as Scholasticism, Aristotelian philosophy became the official philosophy of the Roman Catholic Church.

After Alexander's death, Athens rebelled against Macedonian rule, and Aristotle's political situation became precarious. To avoid being put to death, he fled to the island of Euboea, where he died soon after.

◆◆◆

4

Amadeo Avogadro

(1776-1856)

Italian chemist Amedeo Avogadro found that the atoms in elements combine to form molecules. He proposed that equal volumes of gases under equal conditions of temperature and pressure contain equal numbers of molecules.

Amedeo Avogadro was born August 9, 1776 in Turin, Italy. There was a legal tradition in his family, and in spite of his interest in practical science he studied law and qualified in 1796, being in part-time practice for a long time afterwards.

However, Avogadro also was interested in the natural sciences and in 1800 he began private studies in physics and mathematics. He became Professor of Physics at Vercelli in 1809 and it was here that he produced his famous hypothesis on the volumes of perfect gases. He wrote a memoria (concise note) in which he declared the hypothesis that is now known as Avogadro's law.

Avogadro's law states that equal volumes of gases, at the same temperature and pressure, contain the same number of molecules. His hypothesis wasn't generally accepted until after 1858 (after Avogadro's death), when the Italian chemist Stanislao Cannizzar was able to explain why there were some organic chemical exceptions to Avogadro's hypothesis.

One of the most important contributions of Avogadro's work was his resolution of the confusion surrounding atoms and molecules (although he didn't use the term 'atom'). He believed that particles could be composed of molecules and that molecules could be composed of still simpler units, atoms. The number of molecules in a mole (one gram molecular weight) was termed Avogadro's number (sometimes called Avogadro's constant) in honour of Avogadro's theories. Avogadro's number has been experimentally determined to be 6.023x1023 molecules per gram-mole.

Between 1820 and 1850 he occupied the Chair of Physics at the University of Turin, and conducted research into the electrical properties of substances, as well as making investigations into thermal expansion and specific heat.

Of Avogadro's published works, the most important was his four-volume physics text book, *Fisica dei corpi ponderabili,* which appeared between 1837 and 1841.

Avogadro's fame rests on his proposal that equal volumes of all gases, under the same conditions of temperature and pressure, contain the same number of molecules. This hypothesis was published in 1811 in the French *Journal de Physique,* soon after Gay-Lussac's discovery that the volumes of combining gases bear a simple ratio to each other and to the volume of the new compound.

Avogadro's hypothesis, in conjunction with Gay-Lussac's law, should have allowed the molecular formulae and atomic weights of gases to be determined experimentally, but his paper attracted little attention because it was supported by so little experimental evidence. Avogadro also proposed that the simple gases, such as hydrogen and oxygen, might exist as molecules containing two atoms instead of one, a suggestion that seemed to conflict with the widely-accepted 'indivisible' atomic theory of John Dalton. Avogadro continued to publish papers on the subject, as well as on other chemical research.

The vindication of Avogadro's hypothesis came after his death, when in 1860, Stanislao Cannizzaro presented a system of atomic weights determined using Avogadro's work. Since then his hypothesis has been accepted without question, and his ideas on the molecular nature of the simple gases have also proved to be correct.

He died July 9, 1856 in Turin, Italy.

◆◆◆

5

Charles Babbage

(1792-1871)

Charles Babbage was an English mathematician, philosopher, inventor and mechanical engineer who came up with the concept of a programmable computer and is said to have invented the first mechanical computer.

Charles Babbage was born on December 26, 1791, in Teignmouth, Devonshire, UK.

His father joined a 30-students closed number academy managed by Reverend Stephen Freeman. The academy had a big library, where Babbage used to study mathematics by himself, and learned to love it.

Babbage arrived at Trinity College, Cambridge in October 1810. He was seriously disappointed about the math programmes available there. So he, with J.Herschel, G.Peacock, and other friends, decided to form the Analytical Society. When, in 1812, Babbage transferred to Peterhouse, Cambridge, he was the best mathematician; but he failed to graduate with honours. He received an honorary degree later, without even taking an examination, in 1814.

In Babbage's times there was a really high error rate in the calculation of math tables, when he planned to find a new method that could be use to make it mechanically, removing the human error factor. This idea started to tickle his brain very early, in 1812.

Babbage presented something that he called 'difference engine' to the Royal Astronomical Society on Jun 14, 1822. It was able to calculate polynomials by using a numerical method called the differences method.

Between 1833 and 1842 he tried to build a machine that would be programmable to do any kind of calculation, not just ones relating to polynomial equations. The first break through came when he redirected the machine's output to the input for further equations. In 1824 he won the Gold Medal of the Royal Astronomical Society for his invention of an engine for calculating mathematical and astronomical tables.

From 1828 to 1839 Babbage was Lucasian professor of mathematics at Cambridge. He contributed largely to several scientific periodicals, and was instrumental in founding the Astronomical Society in 1820 and the Statistical Society in 1834.

Charles Babbage also achieved notable results in cryptography. His discovery was used to aid English military campaigns, and was not published until several years later; as a result credit for the development was instead given to Friedrich Kasiski, who made the same discovery some years after Babbage.

In 1838 Babbage also invented the pilot (also called a cow-catcher), the metal frame attached to the front of locomotives that clears the tracks of obstacles. He also performed several studies on Isambard Kingdom Brunel's Great Western Railway.

He is also known for the inventions of the dynamometer, standard railroad gauge, uniform postal rates, occulting lights for lighthouses, Greenwich time signals, heliograph and opthalmoscope.

As the inventor of the first universal digital computer, he can indeed be considered a profound thinker. The use of Jacquard punch cards, of chains and subassemblies, and ultimately the logical structure of the modern computer - all come from Babbage.

His finest work, *On the Economy of Manufactures*, was published in 1832.

He died in 1871 in London.

◆◆◆

6

John Logie Baird

(1888-1946)

John Logie Baird Baird was a Scottish engineer, most famous for being the first person to demonstrate a working television. He pioneered early television with the mechanical scanning system he developed. Among his pioneering ideas were early versions of coluor television, the video disc, large screen television, stereo television, televised sports, and pay television by closed circuit.

Baird was born on 14 August 1888 in Helensburgh on the west coast of Scotland. Dogged by ill health for most of his life, he none the less showed early signs of ingenuity, rigging up a telephone exchange to connect his bedroom to those of his friends across the street. His studies at Glasgow University were interrupted by the outbreak of World War I. Rejected as unfit for the forces, he served as superintendent engineer of the Clyde Valley Electrical Power Company. When the war ended he set himself up in business, with mixed results.

Baird then moved to the south coast of England and applied himself to creating a television, a dream of many scientists for decades. His first crude apparatus was made of odds and ends but by 1924 he managed to transmit a flickering image across a few feet. On 26 January 1926 he gave the world's first demonstration of true television before fifty scientists in an attic room in central London. In 1927 his television was demonstrated over 438 miles of telephone line between London and Glasgow, and he formed the Baird Television Development Company. In

1928 the company achieved the first transatlantic television transmission between London and New York and the first transmission to a ship in mid-Atlantic. He also gave the first demonstration of both colour and stereoscopic television.

Beginning in 1923 and continuing until 1939, Baird produced a series of mechanical video systems that could scan (and thus transmit and receive) moving images. He promoted initial public interest in television with the first public demonstrations in 1925 to 1926, and long-distance transmissions by wire (between London and Glasgow in 1926) and short-wave (trans-Atlantic from London to New York in 1927). By 1928 he was experimenting with 'phonovision', a means of recording his crude images on a phonograph-like disc. His efforts at promotion and sale of 'televisor' devices created considerable controversy among experts as to whether television was sufficiently developed to promote public viewing and purchase of receivers.

For many years, the British Broadcasting Corporation (BBC) resisted his efforts to utilise their frequencies and studio facilities in his work. Under pressure from the British Post Office (then in charge of all wire and wireless transmission), the BBC reluctantly began to work with Baird in 1930. Several years of experiments culminated in a regular daily broadcast comparison of his 240-line system with an RCA-electronic 405-line system developed by Marconi-EMI in 1936-37.

Baird continued developmental work on colour television, now making use of cathode-ray technology, and achieved 600-line experimental colour telecasts by 1940. He continued his effort to perfect large-screen projection colour television during the war, along with some apparent work for the British military. But his health, never strong, gave out and he died in 1946.

◆◆◆

7

Benjamin Banneker

(1731-1806)

Benjamin Banneker, an African American mathematician and amateur astronomer, calculated ephemeredes for almanacs for the years 1792 through 1797 that were widely distributed. A self-taught clockmaker and astronomer, he is also known for his work as an architect and a designer of Washington, D.C.

Benjamin Banneker was born in Maryland on November 9, 1731.

A farmer of modest means, Banneker nevertheless lived a life of unusual achievement. In 1753, the young man borrowed a pocket watch from a well-to-do neighbour; he took it apart and made a drawing of each component, then reassembled the watch and returned it, fully functioning, to its owner.

From his drawings Banneker then proceeded to carve, out of wood, enlarged replicas of each part. Calculating the proper number of teeth for each gear and the necessary relationships between the gears, he constructed a working wooden clock that kept accurate time and struck the hours for over 50 years. His work on the clock led him to repair watches, clocks and sundials. He even helped Joseph Ellicott to build a complex clock.

Banneker became close friends with the Ellicott brothers. They lent him books on astronomy and mathematics as well as instruments for observing the stars. He taught himself astronomy and advanced mathematics

At age 58, Banneker began the study of astronomy and was soon predicting future solar and lunar eclipses. He built a 'work cabin' with a skylight to study the stars and make calculations. Working largely alone, with few visitors, he compiled results which he published in his *Almanac.* He compiled the ephemeris, or information table, for annual almanacs that were published for the years 1792 through 1797. *Benjamin Banneker's Almanac* was a top seller from Pennsylvania to Virginia and even into Kentucky.

In 1791, Banneker was a technical assistant in the calculating and first-ever surveying of the Federal District, which is now Washington, D.C. Major Andrew Ellicott, George Ellicott's cousin, asked Banneker to help him survey the 'Federal Territory'. Banneker and Ellicott worked closely with Pierre L'Enfant who was the architect in charge of planning Washington D.C. L'Enfant was suddenly dismissed from the project, due to his temper. When he left, he took the plans with him. Banneker recreated the plans from memory, saving the U.S. government the effort and expense of having someone else design the capital.

Although Banneker studied and recorded his results until he died, he stopped publishing his *Almanac* due to poor sales. For years he has been referred to as 'the first Negro Man of Science'.

Banneker died on Oct. 9, 1806, and was buried in the family burial ground near his house.

◆◆◆

8

Frederick Grant Banting

(1891-1941)

To millions at home and abroad Frederick Banting was known as the man who discovered insulin, bringing new hope to diabetics the world over. His groundbreaking research in the early 1920s brought him worldwide acclaim and earned him a lifetime annuity from the federal government, a knighthood in the British crown and Canada's first ever Nobel Prize.

Frederick Grant Banting was born on November 14, 1891, at Alliston, Ontario, Canada.

Educated at the Public and High Schools at Alliston, he later went to the University of Toronto to study divinity, but soon transferred to the study of medicine. In 1916 he took his M.B. degree and at once joined the Canadian Army Medical Corps, and served, during the First World War, in France. In 1918 he was wounded at the battle of Cambrai and in 1919 he was awarded the Military Cross for heroism under fire.

When the war ended in 1919, Banting returned to Canada and was for a short time a medical practitioner at London, Ontario. He studied orthopaedic medicine and was, during the year 1919-1920, Resident Surgeon at the Hospital for Sick Children, Toronto. From 1920 until 1921 he did part-time teaching in orthopaedics at the University of Western Ontario at London, Canada, besides his general practice, and from 1921 until 1922 he was Lecturer in Pharmacology at the University of Toronto. In 1922 he was awarded his M.D. degree, together with a gold medal.

After the war, he practised medicine in London, Ontario, until 1921, when he and Charles Best began their research into the hormone insulin. The work progressed rapidly from basic research to clinical application. They discovered the technique for isolating the hormone insulin which is produced in the pancreas. Insulin, when injected, reduces the level of blood sugar and thus relieves the symptoms of diabetes mellitus. This discovery made the treatment of diabetes possible. Banting, along with John J.R. Macleod, head of the physiology department at the University of Toronto, were awarded the Nobel Prize in medicine/physiology in 1923. They were the first Canadians to ever receive this honour.

In the two decades following his discovery Banting struggled to make another similar breakthrough. Despite research into silicosis and cancer, he failed to make any major discoveries. However, he did create the world's first G-suit to help pilots cope with high-speed flight. This led to his appointment in 1939 as the chairman of the National Research Council's Committee on Aviation Medical Research.

Later Banting was named head of a new department of medical research at the University of Toronto, named after him and Charles Best. He became Sir Frederick Banting when he was knighted in 1934.

On February 21, 1941, Banting was killed in a plane crash while on a military medical mission in Newfoundland.

◆◆◆

9

John Bardeen
(1908-1992)

John Bardeen was the inventor of the transistor and leader of the team that developed the microscopic theory of superconductivity. He alongwith Dr. Walter Brattain, and Dr. William Shockley, discovered the transistor effect and developed the first device in December, 1947, while the three were members of the technical staff at Bell Laboratories in Murray Hill, NJ. They were awarded the Nobel Prize in physics in 1956. John Bardeen also received a Nobel Prize for his work on superconductivity.

John Bardeen was born in Madison, Wisconsin on May 23, 1908. He soon displayed formidable mathematical and athletic abilities. After graduating from high school, aged just 13, he took two years of additional high-school courses before starting his undergraduate studies at Wisconsin. He graduated in 1928 despite also having taken a year off during his degree to work in Chicago.

Following two years of graduate work in electrical engineering at Wisconsin — and a three-year spell developing new approaches to oil exploration at Gulf Oil in Pittsburgh — Bardeen went to Princeton as a graduate student in 1933. He completed his PhD on the work function of metals in just two years.

A staff member of the University of Minnesota, Minneapolis, from 1938 to 1941, he served as principal physicist at the US Naval Ordinance Laboratory in Washington, DC, during World War II, after which he joined Bell Telephone Laboratories.in 1945. It was here, working closely with Walter Brattain - his old friend and office-mate - that he invented the transistor in 1947.

Following six years of sustained effort, Bardeen - along with his postdoc Leon Cooper and his graduate student Bob Schrieffer - developed a microscopic theory of the superconductivity of metals at very low temperatures. In the years that followed, as a consultant to Xerox, Bardeen also played a major role in the development of xerography, while continuing to work at Illinois on a wide variety of problems in condensed matter.

Equally important was his total dedication to cracking the problem, and the encouragement, support and freedom to pursue their own ideas that he gave to his younger colleagues, who played key roles in the development of the theory. The resulting BCS theory is arguably one of the major contributions to physics in the 20th century. It not only solved the riddle of superconductivity, but also had a lasting impact on the fields of astrophysics, nuclear physics and particle physics.

Dr. Bardeen died in 1992.

◆◆◆

10

Christiaan Neethling Barnard

(1922-2001)

The South African surgeon, Christiaan N. Barnard, performed the world's first human heart transplant operation in 1967 and the first double-heart transplant in 1974. The patient, 53-year-old dentist Louis Washkansky, was given the heart of a 25-year-old auto crash victim named Denise Darvall. Washkansky died from infection 18 days later, but the transplant made Barnard one of the world's most famous surgeons.

Christiaan N. Barnard was born on November 8, 1922, in Beaufort West, South Africa.

He received his early education in Beaufort West and then went on to the University of Cape Town. He received his M.D. in 1953, before becoming a family physician on the Western Cape.

Barnard worked for a short time as a general practitioner before joining the Cape Town Medical School staff as a research fellow in surgery.

In the years 1953-1955, Barnard had gained recognition for research in gastrointestinal pathology. He proved that the fatal birth defect known as congenital intestinal atresia was due to the foetus receiving an inadequate supply of blood during pregnancy and that it could be remedied by a surgical procedure.

In 1956 he received a Charles Adams Memorial Scholarship and a Dazian Foundation Bursary for a two-year study in the United States of America.

He enrolled at the University of Minnesota Medical School (1955). After two years of study with Dr. Owen H. Wangensteen he received his Ph.D. from Minnesota and returned to his native country to embark upon a career as a cardiothoracic surgeon.

For several years, Barnard experimented with animal heart transplants following the first successful kidney transplant in the US, in 1954. He performed his first kidney transplant in South Africa in 1959.

He continued to work at Groote Schuur Hospital, this time as a specialist in cardiothoracic surgery, and was a full-time lecture and Director of Surgical Research at the University of Cape Town.

He was appointed Head of the Department of Cardiothoracic Surgery at the teaching hospitals at the University of Cape Town.

In 1962, he was promoted to Associate Professor in the Department of Surgery at the University of Cape Town.

He introduced open-heart surgery to that country, designed artificial valves for the human heart, and experimented with the transplantation of the hearts of dogs. By 1967, Barnard was a well respected cardiothoracic surgeon at the Groote Schuur Hospital back in Cape Town, and had already conducted many heart experiments on animals.

Of crucial importance was the first use of hypothermia (artificial lowering of the body temperature) in 1952 and the introduction in the following year of an effective heart-lung machine. These advances, combined with other techniques perfected in the 1960s, enabled a surgeon for the first time to operate upon a heart that was motionless and free of blood.

After a decade of heart surgery, Barnard and his team of cardiac specialists gave the patient Louis Washkansky, a 54-year-old patient who suffered from extensive coronary artery disease large doses of drugs, which allowed the patient's body to accept the new organ. However, Washkansky's body was not able to defend itself against infection, and he died on December 21, 1967 of double pneumonia.Within a year (January 1968) Barnard replaced the diseased heart of Philip Blaiberg, a 58-year-old retired dentist. This time the accompanying drug dosage was lowered, and Blaiberg lived for 20 months with his new heart.

He was promoted to Professor of Surgical Science in the Department of Surgery at the University of Cape Town in 1972.

Seven years after his initial heart transplant, Barnard made medical history once again when he performed a 'twin-heart' operation (November 25, 1974). This time he removed only the diseased portion of the heart of 58-year-old Ivan Taylor and replaced it with the heart of a 10-year-old child. The donor heart acted as a booster and back-up for the patient's disease-ravished organ, but the patient died within four months.

Rheumatoid arthritis forced Barnard to give up surgery in 1983. He retired as Head of the Department of Cardiothoracic Surgery. He spent two years as the Scientist-In-Residence at the Oklahoma Transplantation Institute at the Baptist Medical Center in Oklahoma City in the USA. Over the years he has received many awards over the years, (one of which is the title Professor Emeritus (1984)) the Dag Hammarskjold International Prize and Peace Prize, the Kennedy Foundation Award, and the Milan International Prize for Science. Barnard was also featured in a BBC programme about transplant surgery, in early 1997.

He died in 2001 while vacationing in Cyprus, following an asthma attack.

◆◆◆

11

Sir William Maddock Bayliss

(1860-1924)

Sir William Maddock Bayliss was an English physiologist. He and Ernest Henry Starling discovered the peptide hormone secretin and peristalsis of the intestines. The Bayliss Effect is named after him. He was knighted for his contribution to medicine in 1922.

William Maddock Bayliss was born in Butcroft, Wolverhampton, England, on 2 May, 1860.

He studied at University College, London, and in 1887 graduated from Wadham College, Oxford University. He obtained a first class degree in the School of Natural Science or Physiology. Thereafter he taught physiology at University College, where in 1912 he became professor of physiology. It was here that his great discovery was made.

In 1902, with Ernest H. Starling, he discovered that, when food comes into contact with part of the small intestine, a chemical substance is secreted. This chemical substance is carried via the blood to the pancreas where it stimulates the secretion of pancreatic juice, the most important of the digestive juices. They named this chemical substance secretin. It was the first discovered hormone. They coined the word 'hormone' from the Greek for 'I excite' or 'I arouse'.

Bayliss was elected a fellow of the Royal Society in 1903 and was knighted in 1922.

In 1912 he was appointed Professor of General Physiology at University College. He was awarded the Copley Medal in 1919 for his contributions to science

Amongst his other scientific work Bayliss studied the use of saline injections as a way of counteracting the shock suffered in surgery. He showed how the enzyme trypsin was formed from inactive trypsinogen and measured precisely the time it took to digest protein. As a result of this work he proposed the use of gum-saline injections for wound shock and this was said to have saved many lives of wounded soldiers in the First World War.

In 1915, his classic work *Principles of General Physiology* was published. It ran through four editions in his lifetime.

He was knighted in 1922 and, although he continued to live in Hampstead, he remained a director of the family business, Bayliss, Jones and Bayliss.

Sir William Bayliss died in 1924.

◆◆◆

12

Antoine Henri Becquerel

(1852-1908)

Henri Becquerel was a French physicist who discovered Becquerel rays, the first indications of radio-activity, later named as gamma rays. He shared the Nobel Prize for Physics in 1903 with the Curies.

Antoine Henri Becquerel was born in Paris on December 15, 1852, a member of a distinguished family of scholars and scientists. He was educated at the Lycee Louis-le-Grand,Ecolésar Polytechnique and at the Ecolésar des Ponts et Chaussees, where he received his engineering training.

He entered the Polytechnic in 1872, then the government department of Ponts-et-Chaussées in 1874, becoming ingénieur in 1877 and being promoted to ingénieur-en-chef in 1894. In 1888 he acquired the degree of docteur-ès-sciences.

From 1878 he had held an appointment as an Assistant at the Museum of Natural History, taking over from his father in the Chair of Applied Physics at the Conservatoire des Arts et Metiers. In 1892 he was appointed Professor of Applied Physics in the Department of Natural History at the Paris Museum. He became a Professor at the Polytechnic in 1895.

Becquerel's earliest work was concerned with the plane polarisation of light, with the phenomenon of phosphorescence and with the absorption of light by crystals. He also worked on the subject of terrestrial magnetism.

In 1896, his previous work was overshadowed by his discovery of the phenomenon of natural radioactivity. Following a discussion with Henri Poincaré on the radiation which had recently been discovered by Röntgen (X-rays) and which was accompanied by a type of phosphorescence in the vacuum tube, Becquerel decided to investigate whether there was any connection between X-rays and naturally occurring phosphorescence. He had inherited from his father a supply of uranium salts, which phosphoresce on exposure to light. When the salts were placed near to a photographic plate covered with opaque paper, the plate was discovered to be fogged. The phenomenon was found to be common to all the uranium salts studied and was concluded to be a property of the uranium atom. Later, he showed that the rays emitted by uranium, which for a long time were named after their discoverer, caused gases to ionise and that they differed from X-rays in that they could be deflected by electric or magnetic fields.

Initially he believed that the sun's energy was being absorbed by the uranium which then emitted X rays. Further investigation, on 26 and 27 of February, was delayed because the skies over Paris were overcast and the uranium-covered plates Becquerel intended to expose to the sun were returned to a drawer. On the first of March, he developed the photographic plates expecting only faint images to appear. To his surprise, the images were clear and strong. This meant that the uranium emitted radiation without an external source of energy such as the sun. Becquerel had discovered radioactivity, the spontaneous emission of radiation by a material. Later, he demonstrated that the radiation emitted by uranium shared certain characteristics with X rays but, unlike X rays, could be deflected by a magnetic field and therefore must consist of charged particles. For his discovery of radioactivity, Becquerel was awarded the1903 Nobel Prize for physics.

Antoine Henri Becquerel died at Le Croisic on August 25, 1908.

◆◆◆

13

Alexander Graham Bell

(1847-1922)

Alexander Graham Bell was a pioneer in the field of telecommunications. He was an eminent scientist, inventor and innovator, credited with inventing the first practical telephone.

Alexander Graham Bell was born on March 3, 1847 in Edinburgh, Scotland. In 1870, Bell and his family moved to Ontario, and then to the United States. He settled down in Boston, before beginning his career as an inventor.

As a child Alexander Bell was interested in many things, he always kept wondering. One thing he was interested in was sounds and tones. Because of his interest, he played piano; in fact he played quite well. He was also especially interested in speech. He even did experiments on his dog by pressing gently on the dog's voice box to make it sound like someone was talking. He had a special love for science. As a child he would bring home animals to study and dissect.

When he was only sixteen he taught music. During his teachings, he would experiment with tuning forks, vibrating the prongs. After his experiments, he thought, if the vibration of sound could be sent on metal prongs, couldn't he send speech on a wire?

He soon made a few close friends who would help him. Mr. Sanders and Mr. Hubbard were Bell's financial backers. They would give him money and a room to experiment, and would get a share of the eventual profits. Alexander and another friend,

Tom Watson, would work endlessly during the evenings. They worked with tuning forks, wires, batteries and electromagnets. Thanks to Alexander's sharp ear, they could make adjustments more precisely.

During the previous summer, in 1874, he figured out what would make speech go across the wire. He had the basic idea of the telephone. Most nights ended in disappointment, but on June 2, 1875, Watson sent vibration from one room, and Bell received it from another room. After what had happened, Bell was sure speech could be sent. The telephone was now on its way.

Watson and Bell took the telephone idea and made it a product. It took time, hard work and patience. They experimented all summer and had set aside the multiple telegraph. They could now send messages over the phone, however nothing was understood on the other end. Since it was still unclear, they made another transmitter. This transmitter was made with a wire connected to a metal cup that was filled with diluted sulfuric acid. It was now the 10th of March in 1876. Tom got the telephone ready to test. He picked up the receiver and placed it to his ear. Moments later, the first telephone message had been sent. By 1878, he had set up the first telephone exchange in New Haven, Connecticut. By 1884, long distance connections were made between Boston, Massachusetts and New York City.

Bell continued his experiments in communication. He invented the photophone-transmission of sound on a beam of light, which was a precursor of fibre-optics. He also invented techniques for teaching speech to the deaf. He was granted 18 patents in his name, and 12 he shared with collaborators. He also founded the National Geographic Society in 1888.

Alexander Graham Bell died in Baddek, Nova Scotia, on August 2, 1922.

◆◆◆

14

Karl Benz
(1844-1929)

Karl Friedrich Benz was the German engine designer and automobile engineer who invented the gasoline-powered automobile. It was a three-wheeler; Benz built his first four-wheeled car in 1891. Benz & Company, the company started by the inventor, became the world's largest manufacturer of automobiles by 1900.

Karl Friedrich Benz was born in 1844 in Baden Muehlburg, Germany. He attended the Karlsruhe grammar school and later the Karlsruhe Polytechnic University. In 1871, he founded his first company with partner August Ritter, the Iron Foundry and Machine Shop, a supplier of building materials.

Benz began his work on a two-stroke engine, in hopes of finding a new income. He received his first patent in 1879. In 1883, he founded Benz & Company to produce industrial engines in Mannheim, Germany. He then began designing a motor carriage, with a four-stroke engine (based on Nicolaus Otto's patent).

Benz designed his engine and the body for the three-wheel vehicle with an electric ignition, differential gears, and water-cooling. The vehicle was powered by a water cooled gas engine that was driven by the vapour of ligroin, or benzine. The rear wheels received the power by a pulley and belt that were attached to a transmission shaft whilst the water cooling was by water evaporation in a jacket round the cylinder. The car was first driven in Mannheim in 1885. On January 29, 1886, he was granted a patent for his gas-fueled automobile and in July, he began selling his automobile to the public.

Accepted as the inventor of the motor car Karl Benz first unveiled his Benz 3-wheeler in 1885 at Mannheim. (Germany). He unveiled the Motorwagen, a three-wheeler powered by a four-stroke gasoline engine. It was the first ever commercial automobile.

Despite inventors like Gottlieb Daimler who worked on 4-wheeler designs, Benz stuck to a 3-wheeled design for many years producing many vehicles but in the days before tarmac roads, many common place roads consisted of two rutted tracks left by horse drawn coaches. Whilst the 4-wheeler would often run in these ruts the front wheel of a 3-wheeler was running on uneven ground creating a bumpy ride and placing great stress on the structure of the vehicle itself. Benz had initially designed his vehicle as a 3-wheeler to overcome problems with steering.

In 1888 Benz started to advertise his 3-wheeler but the public refused to buy it. It was after his family (his wife and two sons) stole the car one night and drove it from Mannheim to Pforzheim (approximately 65 miles) that the public became fascinated by it and the Benz started to sell. From 1893 Benz then changed his vehicle to a 4-wheeled design (The Benz Viktoria). He then later merged with Daimler to become Daimler-Benz. or Mercedes-Benz as most people know of it today, The name 'Mercedes' came from one of Daimler's business partners, Emil Jellinek.

And true to his legendary status, the automotive legacy of Karl Benz is far from limited to engine construction. The avid engine designer and inventor kept true to his passion and received patents for numerous other related inventions, including accelerators, spark plugs and carburettors.

In 1903, Karl Benz retired from Benz & Company; his designs were already outdated by Gottlieb Daimler. He served as a member of the supervisory board of Daimler-Benz AG from 1926, when the company was formed, until his death.

Benz passed away in 1929.

◆◆◆

15

Homi Jehangir Bhabha

(1909-1966)

Widely referred to as the father of India's nuclear weapons programme, Homi Jehangir Bhabha was a famous Indian nuclear physicist who founded the Tata Institute of Fundamental Research; was the first chairman of India's Atomic Energy Commissin; and was chairman of the first United Nations Conference on the Peaceful Uses of Atomic Energy, held in Geneva in 1955.

Homi Jehangir Bhabha was born on October 30, 1909, in Bombay in a rich Parsi family.

After studying at the Cathedral High School in Bombay, Bhabha had his education at the Elphinstone College and the Royal Institute of Science, Bombay.

He proceeded to England, in 1927, to join the Caius College in Cambridge to study engineering, but his heart was really in physics. And so, immediately after passing the Mechanical Sciences Tripos in 1930, he switched over to research in theoretical physics. He obtained his doctorate from the University of Cambridge in 1934.

During the period 1930-1939, Bhabha carried out outstanding original research relating to cosmic radiation, coming up with observations on the production of electron pairs in the interaction of cosmic radiation with matter, and also identifying muons — heavier than electron particles — as present in the penetrating component of cosmic rays. All this earned for him his election to the prestigious Fellowship of the Royal Society in 1940, at the young age of 31.

He was influenced greatly by the legendary Paul Dirac. Bhabha was a research scientist at the Cavendish Laboratories at Cambridge. He worked with Niels Bohr on the studies that led to quantum theory. He also worked with Walter Heitler on the cascade theory of electron showers, which was of great importance for the understanding of cosmic radiation. He did significant work in identifying the meson.

Due to outbreak of the Second World War, Bhabha returned to India in 1939. He set up the Cosmic Ray Research Unit at the Indian Institute of Science, Bangalore under Nobel Laureate C. V. Raman in 1939. With the help of J.R.D. Tata, he established the Tata Institute of Fundamental Research at Mumbai. In 1945, he became director of the Tata Institute of Fundamental Research.

Apart from being a great scientist, Homi Bhabha was also a skilled administrator. After independence he established the Atomic Energy Commission of India in 1948. Under his guidance Indian scientists worked on the development of atomic energy, and the first atomic reactor in Asia went into operation at Trombay, near Bombay, in 1956.

Homi Bhabha was chairman of the first United Nations Conference on the Peaceful Uses of Atomic Energy, held in Geneva in 1955. He advocated international control of nuclear energy and the outlawing of atomic bombs by all countries. He wanted nuclear energy to be used for alleviating poverty and misery of people.

Homi Bhabha received many honorary degrees from Indian and foreign universities and was a member of numerous scientific societies, including the National Academy of Sciences in the United States. He also authored many articles on quantum theory and cosmic rays.

The atomic energy centre in Trombay was renamed as Bhabha Atomic Research Centre in his honour.

Homi Bhabha died in an aeroplane crash near Mont Blanc in Switzerland on January 24, 1966.

◆◆◆

16

Forrest Bird

(1921-)

Forrest Bird is best known as the inventor of the first practical mass-produced medical respirator. Often called the 'Babybird' respirator, this wonderful device reduced infant death drastically across the world.

Forrest Bird was born in Stoughton, Massachusetts in 1921.

He learned to fly a plane with the encouragement of his father, a World War I pilot. By the age of fourteen in 1935, young Forrest was soloed by his father in his 1928 Waco Biplane. In 1941, with extensive aviation qualifications, he was called to active duty as a Technical Air Training Officer in the US Army Air Corps.

During World War II, as a highly qualified pilot, Forrest transitioned almost every aircraft the Armed Services had in inventory. He was one of the earliest military Jet as well as Helicopter pilots. At that time, new designs in airplanes allowed for flight at higher altitudes; however, gear was now needed that would allow pilots to breathe at a higher altitude. These experiences began Forrest Bird lifelong research into respirators. He studied medicine and became a doctor.

Over the years, Forrest Bird developed Aircrew Breathing Regulators and anti "g" devices. After an Air Corps physician presented him textbooks on mammalian pathophysiology, he became a lifelong student of the subject.

Bird attended a number of medical schools and completed several residencies. This knowledge eventually led him to develop the prototype Bird Universal Medical Respirator for acute or chronic cardiopulmonary care.

Bird founded Bird Products Corporation in 1954 to market and develop his device. Beginning in 1958, he tested it by traveling to medical schools; there he would ask doctors for their most ill patients, for whom known therapies had failed and death by cardiopulmonary failure was expected.

His testing allowed him to make important improvements on his designs. His small, green box-like apparatus quickly became a common piece of equipment in hospitals around the world. In 1970, Bird introduced the 'Babybird' respirator, which reduced infant mortality due to respirator problems from 70 per cent to less than 10 per cent.

Today, over 40 years later, Bird Products is part of Thermo Electron's division of biomedical companies. Bird Products is considered a worldwide leader in the respiratory care industry and has continued advancement in technologies that offer the greatest clinical benefit to patients.

Based on the research conducted by its founder, Bird Products has developed a number of advanced breathing-related medical devices and technologies, and Dr. Bird himself continues to be very active in contributing to the team's work. The V.I.P Bird Infant Pediatric System was introduced in 1992, specifically designed for the neonatal, infant and pediatric patient population. The TBird Ventilator Series is the world's first and only ventilator that can move with the patient from each clinical setting to the next without interruption.

By the 1980s, Forrest Bird invented the Intrapulmonary Percussive Ventilation or IPV, a major advance in mechanical cardiopulmonary care.

In 1995 Dr. Bird was inducted into the US Inventors Hall of Fame for his developments in fluid Dynamics and the patented BABYbird. He is a past president of the Civil Aviation Medical Association (CAMA).

Dr. Bird is still an active highly qualified FAA certificated Flight Instructor Pilot and Aeronautical Engineer. He remains an ardent Lecturer as well as Educator, with deep Research and Development commitments in Aeromedicine.

◆◆◆

17

Laszlo Biro

(1899-1985)

Bíro, a Hungarian Jew, invented the now-ubiquitous ballpoint pen. He invented other things but his name will be for ever associated with the ballpoint pen, in fact in Britain a ballpoint pen is usually referred to as a 'Bíro'.

László Bíró was born in Budapest on September 19, 1899. He gained a place at the Medical School in Budapest but did not graduate. For a time he dabbled with hypnosis then he got a job with an oil company as a clerk responsible for matters relating to customs duties. He also had a go at motor racing, which provided the stimulus for his next invention — a new type of gear lever. He was also a successful painter.

Bíro was always a tinkerer, and in addition to his pen he held patents for a steam-powered washing machine and an automatic transmission for cars.

The need to invent something like the ballpoint pen arose when he took up journalism. He was the editor of the journal *Hongrie-Magyarország-Hungary* and when this was closed down he began working for the newspaper *Elôtte*. As a journalist he was frequently irritated by the difficulties involved in using a fountain pen and began to think about how he could replace it with a more convenient writing implement.

It was during his time here that he was impressed by the ink used in the newspaper printers; it was extremely quick-drying and hardly smudged at all. At the time, fountain pens were the best writing instrument available, but they were messy and inconvenient, and blotting paper had to be used to ensure that the India ink they used wasn't unwittingly smeared across the page. Biro was inspired to create a pen with thicker, quick-drying ink that would remedy all of these problems.

Eventually he realised that the technique used in printing by which a rotary cylinder ensures continuous and uniform application of the ink could be adapted for use in a pen in such a way that a slender tube filled with ink with a small ball bearing at the end would be able to apply the ink continuously to the paper. He enlisted the help of his brother, George, who was a chemist, to try and find a ink that would work in such a pen, and in 1938, the two brothers took out their first ballpoint pen patent. It took several years of experimentation, however before the original idea could be realised in the form of the ballpoint pen, which rapidly became popular all over the world. Part of this experimentation was carried out abroad because in 1939 fears for his own and his family's safety prompted him to flee from Hungary, firstly to Paris and then to Argentina.

In 1940, in Argentina, Laszlo Bíro began experimenting independently until he finally patented his ballpoint pen there in 1943. The first ballpoint pens sold in large numbers to the public were manufactured in 1945 and were marketed in Argentina under the name of 'Eterpen'.

Laszlo Bíro was so highly respected in Argentina that the Argentine Inventors' Day is celebrated on his birthday, September 29th.

He is most famous for lending his name to the pen he invented, but he also is credited for designing a reliable automatic gearbox, which he sold to the Ford Motor Company. Unfortunately for him, this commercial success wasn't a theme throughout his life, as he failed to capitalise on the good ideas he and his brother, George, conceived.

Laszlo Bíro died on November 24, 1985 in Buenos Aires.

◆◆◆

18

Niels Henrik David Bohr

(1885-1962)

Niels Henrik David Bohr was a Danish physicist who made fundamental contributions to understanding atomic structure and quantum mechanics, for which he received the Nobel Prize in Physics in 1922.

Niels Henrik David Bohr was born in Copenhagen on October 7, 1885. He finished his matriculation at the Gammelholm Grammar School in 1903, specialising in mathematics and physics. He entered Copenhagen University, and took his Master's degree in Physics in 1909 and his Doctor's degree in 1911. He then travelled to Manchester, England to study under Ernest Rutherford.

While still a student, the announcement by the Academy of Sciences in Copenhagen of a prize to be awarded for the solution of a certain scientific problem, caused him to take up an experimental and theoretical investigation of the surface tension by means of oscillating fluid jets. This work, which he carried out in his father's laboratory and for which he received the prize offered (a gold medal), was published in the *Transactions of the Royal Society*, 1908.

In the autumn of 1911 at Cambridge, he profited by following the experimental work going on in the Cavendish Laboratory under Sir J.J. Thomson's guidance and at the same time as he pursued own theoretical studies.

In the spring of 1912 he was at work in Professor Rutherford's laboratory in Manchester. Having there carried out a theoretical piece of work on the absorption of alpha rays which was published in the *Philosophical Magazine*, 1913, he passed on to a study of the structure of atoms on the basis of Rutherford's discovery of the atomic nucleus.

By introducing conceptions borrowed from the Quantum Theory as established by Planck, he succeeded in working out and presenting a picture of atomic structure that, with later improvements, still fitly serves as an elucidation of the physical and chemical properties of the elements.

Bohr also described the way atoms emit radiation by suggesting that when an electron jumps from an outer orbit to an inner one, that it emits light. Later other physicists expanded his theory into quantum mechanics. This theory explains the structure and actions of complex atoms.

In 1913-1914 Bohr held a Lectureship in Physics at Copenhagen University and in 1914-1916 a similar appointment at the Victoria University in Manchester. In 1916 he was appointed Professor of Theoretical Physics at Copenhagen University, and since 1920 (until his death in 1962) he was at the head of the Institute of Theoretical Physics, established for him at that university.

Bohr became a Fellow of the Royal Society of London in 1926, receiving the Royal Society Copley Medal in 1938.

Recognition of his work on the structure of atoms came with the award of the Nobel Prize for 1922.

Bohr also contributed to the clarification of the problems encountered in quantum physics, in particular by developing the concept of complementarity.

Bohr spent the last two years of World War II in England and America, where he became associated with the Atomic Energy Project. In his later years, he devoted his work to the peaceful application of atomic physics and to political problems arising from the development of atomic weapons.

Bohr received the first U.S. Atoms for Peace Award in 1957.

Niels Bohr died in Copenhagen on November 18, 1962.

19

Ludwig Boltzmann

(1844-1906)

Ludwig Boltzmann, an Austrian physicist, mathematician and philosopher, was a pioneer of quantum mechanics. In his statistical interpretation of the second law of thermodynamics he introduced the theory of probability into a fundamental law of physics and thus broke with the classical prejudice, that fundamental laws have to be strictly deterministic.

Ludwig Eduard Boltzmann was born on February 20, 1844 in Vienna, Austria.

Boltzmann studied at Vienna University from 1863 to 1866. Although Boltzmann's first scientific paper was on electrodynamics, his second was devoted to the mechanical meaning of the second law of thermodynamics - to which he eventually gave an exhaustive answer.

Boltzmann was awarded a doctorate from the University of Vienna in 1866. He became an assistant to his teacher Josef Stefan. He taught at Graz, moved to Heidelberg and then to Berlin.

By the time he was 25 years old, Boltzmann was already a full professor of mathematical physics at the University of Graz. In 1890 he moved to the University of Munich, where he was able to devote his lectures entirely to theoretical physics. He enjoyed the academic life at Munich, but the university could not provide for his retirement, so in 1895 he moved back to Vienna to succeed Stefan. However, he soon regretted that decision, and in 1900 left for the University of Leipzig. He did not last long there either, and within two years was back in Vienna once more.

Boltzmann obtained the Maxwell-Boltzmann distribution in 1871, namely, the average energy of motion of a molecule is the same for each direction. He argued that the equipartition theorem was a fundamental feature of the kinetic theory. He also derived the 'H-theorem' and Boltzmann equation in his paper of 1872. The H-theorem expresses the increase in entropy of an irreversible process.

Boltzmann developed his statistical interpretation of the second law of thermodynamics in his famous paper of 1877 on the second law and probability calculus. It was in this paper that Boltzmann's famous relation, S = k log W, first appeared. This equation links the entropy, S, to the logarithm of the number of microstates, W, that a given macroscopic state of the system can have, with k now being known as Boltzmann's constant. Since W is proportional to the probability of the macroscopic state, then the equilibrium state is by far the most probable. The transition from a non-equilibrium to the equilibrium state is simply a transition from a very improbable to the most probable state. This relationship — was later called Boltzmann's principle by Einstein. It is also engraved on Boltzmann's tombstone in Vienna.

Boltmann's greatness was recognised during his lifetime. He was honoured nationally and internationally. He was elected to membership or honorary membership in many academies, received an honorary doctorate from Oxford, and was also awarded medals.

Attacks on his work continued and he began to feel that his life's work was about to collapse despite his defence of his theories. Depressed and in bad health, Boltzmann committed suicide in September 1906 just before experiment verified his work.

◆◆◆

20

Sir Jagadish Chandra Bose

(1885-1962)

Jagadish Chandra Bose was an eminent Indian scientist. He was the first to prove that plants and metals too have feelings. He was a pioneer in microwave optics technology. He was the first to show that semiconductor rectifiers could detect radio waves. His galena receiver was amongst the earliest examples of a lead sulphide photo conducting device.

Jagadish Chandra Bose was born on November 30, 1858 in Mymensingh (now in Bangladesh). He had his early education in a Bengal medium school . In 1869, he was sent to Calcutta to learn English and was educated at St.Xavier's School and College. He was a brilliant student. He passed the B.A. in physical sciences in 1879.

In 1880, Bose went to study medicine at London University, England, for a year but gave it up because of his own ill health. Within a year he moved to Cambridge to take up a scholarship to study Natural Science at Christ's College Cambridge. In 1885, he returned from abroad with a B.Sc. degree and Natural Science Tripos.

Bose was offered lectureship at Presidency College, Calcutta.

In 1894, Bose decided to devote himself to pure research. He converted a small enclosure adjoining a bathroom in the Presidency College into a laboratory. He carried out experiments involving refraction, diffraction and polarisation. To receive the radiation, he used a variety of different junctions connected to a highly sensitive galvanometer. He plotted in detail the voltage-current characteristics of his junctions, noting their non-linear characteristics. He developed the use of galena crystals for making receivers, both for short wavelength radio waves and for white and ultraviolet light. Patent rights for their use in detecting electromagnetic radiation were granted to him in 1904.

In 1954 Pearson and Brattain gave priority to Bose for the use of a semi-conducting crystal as a detector of radio waves.

In 1895 Bose gave his first public demonstration of electromagnetic waves, using them to ring a bell remotely and to explode some gunpowder.

During the years 1894-1900, Bose performed pioneering research on radio waves and created waves as short as 5 mm. Unlike Marconi who sought to commercialise his work with radio waves, Bose was purely interested in radio waves as a scientific endeavour.

Bose was the first to use a semiconductor junction to detect radio waves, and he invented various now commonplace microwave components. Outside of India he is rarely given the deserved recognition.

Bose later switched from physics to the study of metals and then plants. He fabricated a highly sensitive 'coherer', the device that detects radio waves. He found that the sensitivity of the coherer decreased when it was used continuously for a long period and it regained its sensitivity when he gave the device some rest. He thus concluded that metals have feelings and memory.

Bose showed experimentally plants too have life. He invented an instrument to record the pulse of plants and connected it to a plant. The plant, with its roots, was carefully picked up and dipped up to its stem in a vessel containing bromide, a poison. The plant's pulse beat, which the instrument recorded as a steady to-and-fro movement like the pendulum of a clock, began to grow unsteady. Soon, the spot vibrated violently and then came to a sudden stop. The plant had died because of poison.

He studied the effects of electromagnetic radiation on plants, a topical field today. His contributions to this field were pioneering. He introduced many delicate and sensitive instruments, such as the Chrestograph, which was used for recording plant growth. It could magnify a small movement as much as a million times. Another device he developed demonstrated the effects of electromagnetic waves on living and nonliving matter.

It is now recognised that Bose had made very significant contributions to the field of chronobiology and circadian rhythms even before these two technical terms were coined.

Although Bose did invaluable work in science, his work was recognised in the country only when the Western world recognised its importance. He retired in 1915 and was appointed Emeritus Professor, Presidency College, Calcutta, for a period of five years. He founded the Bose Institute at Calcutta, which was the first scientific research institute in India, devoted mainly to the study of plants. Today, the Institute carries research on other fields too.

In 1917 a knighthood was conferred on Bose. In 1920 he became the first Indian scientist to be elected to Great Britain's prestigious Royal Society.

Jagadish Chandra Bose died on November 23, 1937.

◆◆◆

21

Satyendra Nath Bose

(1894-1974)

Satyendra Nath Bose was an Indian physicist specialising in mathematical physics. He is best known for his work on quantum mechanics in the early 1920s, providing the foundation for Bose-Einstein statistics and the theory of the Bose-Einstein condensate. He is honoured as the namesake of the boson.

Satyendra Nath Bose was born on January 1, 1894 in Calcutta. He had his schooling from Hindu High School in Calcutta. It was here that his interest in mathematics and science began. He passed the ISC in 1911 from the Presidency College, Calcutta securing the first position. He did his B.Sc. in Mathematics from the Presidency College in 1913 and M.Sc. in Mixed Mathematics in 1915 from the same college. He topped the university in B.Sc. and M.Sc. Exams.

He continued to study physics and mathematics and was appointed to the newly opened University College of Science in Calcutta in 1917. Here Bose was able to study recent European texts on quantum theory and relativity which, before the opening of the new institution, had not been readily available in India. Gibbs's book on statistical mechanics stimulated Bose's interest in this topic. He also studied Einstein's papers on relativity and obtained Einstein's permission to translate them for publication in India.

Bose was appointed as a Reader in physics at the University of Dacca in 1921 and taught there until 1945, being a professor and head of the physics department from 1927.

His work ranged over many aspects of physics, among them statistical mechanics, the electromagnetic properties of the ionosphere, theories of x-ray crystallography, and unified field theory. However it is for his work in quantum statistics that he is best known.

In 1924, Bose published an article titled 'Max Planck's Law and Light Quantum Hypothesis'. This article was sent to Albert Einstein. Einstein appreciated it so much that he himself translated it into German and sent it for publication to a famous periodical in Germany. The hypothesis received a great attention and was highly appreciated by the scientists. It became famous to the scientists as 'Bose-Einstein Theory'. As a result his application to the University of Dacca for two years research leave beginning in 1924 was approved. While he was in Berlin he attended a course on quantum theory given by Born.

In 1929 Bose was elected chairman of the Physics of the Indian Science Congress and in 1944 elected full chairman of the Congress.

In 1945 he returned to Calcutta University when he was appointed as Gurprasad Sing Professor of Physics, a position he held until he retired in 1956 when he was made Professor Emeritus.

He gave leadership in many ways: as president of the physics section of the Indian Science Congress in 1939, as general president of the Indian Science Congress in Delhi in 1944, and as president of the National Institute of Science of India in 1949.

After Bose retired from Calcutta University in 1956 he was appointed as vice-chancellor of Viswa-Bharati University, Santiniketan. Two years later he was honoured with the post of national professor.

In 1958, he was made a Fellow of the Royal Society, London.

Satyendra Nath Bose was honoured with Padma Bhusan by the Indian Government in recognition of his outstanding achievement.

He died in Kolkata on February 4, 1974.

◆◆◆

22

Robert Boyle

(1627-1691)

Robert Boyle was an Anglo-Irish physicist and chemist, often referred to as the father of modern chemistry. It was Boyle who separated chemistry from alchemy and gave the first precise definitions of a chemical element, a chemical reaction, and chemical analysis. He assembled what we would today call a 'research group', developed the vacuum pump and used it in the discovery of what has become known as Boyle's law. He was instrumental in founding the Royal Society.

Robert Boyle was born on 27 January 1627 in County Waterford in the south-east of Ireland. He was educated at Eton and then in Europe. He returned in 1644 extremely interested in science and settled in Dorset where he built a laboratory.

In 1655 or 1666 Boyle moved to Oxford. It was here that he engaged Robert Hooke as an assistant and together they devised the most famous piece of experimental equipment associated with Boyle, the vacuum chamber or air-pump. Boyle's pump could be operated easily and efficiently by one man. With it he demonstrated that the sound of a bell in the receiver faded as the air was removed, proving that air was necessary for the transmission of sound. In further experiments, he also proved that air was necessary for life and for a candle flame.

He made important contributions to physics and chemistry and is best known for Boyle's law (sometimes called Mariotte's Law) describing an ideal gas. Boyle's law appears in an appendix written in 1662 to his work *New Experiments Physio-Mechanical., Touching the Spring of the Air and its Effects* (1660). The 1660 text was the result of three years of experimenting with an air pump with the help of Hooke. The apparatus had been designed by Hooke and using it Boyle had discovered a whole series of important facts. In performing the experiments which led to this generalization, Boyle had shown, among other things, that sound did not travel in a vacuum, he had proved that flame required air as did life, and he investigated the elastic properties of air.

He was the first prominent scientist to perform controlled experiments and publish his work with details concerning procedure, apparatus and observations. He began to publish in 1659 and continued to do so for the rest of his life on subjects as diverse as philosophy, medicine and religion.

Boyle's empiricism established him as a founder of the modern scientific method and his arguments were so persuasive as to win many important converts, most notably Isaac Newton.

Boyle was a founding fellow of the Royal Society. In 1654, Boyle had joined a small group of the most influential English scientists, mathematicians, philosophers and physicians who had been meeting weekly in London and in Oxford since 1645. In 1662 the group was chartered as the Royal Society which exists today as the oldest continuous scientific society in the world..

He published his results on the physical properties of air through this Society. Although others before him had applied mathematics to physics, Boyle was one of the first to extend the application of mathematics to chemistry which he tried to develop as a science whose complex appearance was merely the result on simple mathematical laws applied to simple fundamental particles.

In 1680, Boyle was elected president of the Royal Society, but declined the honour because the required oath violated his religious principles.

Robert Boyle died in London on December 30, 1691.

◆◆◆

23

Louis Braille

(1894-1974)

Louis Braille, a French educationist, was the inventor of Braille, a world-wide system used by blind and visually impaired people for reading and writing. He also went on to lay the foundations of the braille representation of music, and in 1829 published the "Method of Writing Words, Music and Plain Song by Means of Dots, for Use by the Blind and Arranged by Them".

Louis was born on January 4 in 1809 in Coupvray, France. In 1812, he became blind at the age of three, when he was trying to cut leather with an awl in his father's saddle shop a couple miles out of Paris, France. But, the awl slipped and went into his eye. An injury to his eye at age three resulted in total loss of vision in both eyes.

Seven years later, on February 15, 1819, his family sent him off to the National Institute for Blind Children where he then surpassed his classmates and began to play the piano and the organ.

Then in 1821, a former soldier named Charles Barbier visited the school. He shared his invention called 'night writing', a code of 12 raised dots that let soldiers share top-secret information on the battlefield without even having to speak. Unfortunately, the code was too hard for the soldiers, but not for 12-year-old Louis!

For use in writing his system, he had the device Barbier had used to write sonography — a grooved slate to hold the paper, and a sliding ruler to guide the stylus. The ruler was pierced by little windows. By positioning the stylus in these openings, a blind person could punch dots across the page with precession, then slide the ruler down to the next line. The stylus produces depressions on the paper. One must therefore write from right to left and turn over the paper in order to read it.

At age 15, Louis completed his first dot alphabet by getting up in the middle of the night and working on his invention, but then falling asleep during class! He wanted to work by himself, not with other people, but alone. Some characteristics that enabled him to invent Braille were that he was blind, he was determined, and he didn't want to read the big books that the school gave to their students.

Louis trimmed Barbier's 12 dots into 6, ironed out the system by the time he was 15, then published the first-ever braille book in 1829 and revised it in 1837, including all the letters of the French alphabet (W was added later), punctuation, mathematical symbols, and even musical notation was in there.

In 1837, he added symbols for math and music. But since the public was sceptical, blind students had to study braille on their own.

With this system, Louis swept away all the shortcomings of embossing. The raised-dot characters were simple and complete. They could read quickly with a touch of a finger. They took up little space than conventional printed letters. The Braille system, as it came to be known, made it possible to place the world's literature at the fingertips of blind people.

After Louis graduated from the Royal Institution, he decided to become a teacher there.

Even here, braille wasn't taught until after his death. Braille began to spread worldwide in 1868, when a group of British men, now known as the Royal National Institute for the Blind, took up the cause.

Now practically every country in the world uses braille. Louis proved that if you have the motivation, you can do incredible things.

Louis Braille died at age forty-three, confident that his mission on earth was completed.

24

Brahmagupta

(598-668)

Brahmagupta was the foremost Indian mathematician and astronomer of his time. He made advances in astronomy and most importantly in number systems including algorithms for square roots and the solution of quadratic equations.

Brahmagupta was born in 598 in Gujarat in the city of Bhinmal that is presently in North West Rajasthan.

He was the head of the department of mathematics and astronomy at the university set up by another great Vedic Indian mathematician Aryabhata at the city of Ujjain which was at that time a great center for learning science, literature, Sanskrit and the art of prediction called astronomy.

He became the head of the astronomical observatory at Ujjain the foremost mathematical centre of ancient India then. Outstanding mathematicians such as Varahamihira had worked there and built up a strong school of mathematical astronomy.

He wrote important works on mathematics and astronomy. In particular he wrote *Brahmasphutasiddhanta* (The Opening of the Universe), in 628. The book contains twenty-five chapters but the first ten of these chapters seem to form what many historians believe was a first version of his work and some manuscripts exist which contain only these chapters. These ten chapters are arranged in topics which are typical of Indianmathematical astronomy texts of the period.

The topics covered are: mean longitudes of the planets; true longitudes of the planets; the three problems of diurnal rotation; lunar eclipses; solar eclipses; risings and settings; the moon's crescent; the moon's shadow; conjunctions of the planets with each other; and conjunctions of the planets with the fixed stars.

The remaining fifteen chapters seem to form a second work which is major addendum to the original treatise. The chapters are: examination of previous treatises on astronomy; on mathematics; additions to chapters 1-5; additions to chapter 7; on algebra; on the gnomon; on meters; on the sphere; on instruments; summary of contents; versified tables.

Brahmagupta's understanding of the number systems went far beyond that of others of the period. In the *Brahmasphutasiddhanta* he defined zero as the result of subtracting a number from itself. When zero is added to a number or subtracted from a number, the number remains unchanged; and a number multiplied by zero becomes zero. He also gives arithmetical rules in terms of fortunes (positive numbers) and debts (negative numbers).:

Brahmagupta then tried to extend arithmetic to include division by zero: Positive or negative numbers when divided by zero is a fraction the zero as denominator. Zero divided by negative or positive numbers is either zero or is expressed as a fraction with zero as numerator and the finite quantity as denominator. Zero divided by zero is zero.

Another arithmetical result presented by Brahmagupta is his algorithm for computing square roots. In chapter 12 he promulgates five types of fraction combinations.

He gives the sum of the squares of the first n natural numbers as $n(n+1)(2n+1)/6$ and the sum of the cubes of the first n natural numbers as $(n(n+1)/2)$

Brahmagupta developed some algebraic notation and presents methods to solve quardatic equations. He gave three formulas

1) X=e-c / b-d
2) X=v4ac+b2 -b/2a
3) X=vac+b2 /4-b/2

The basic difference between these simplified formulates and the original ones is that he placed numbers side by side for addition and dots for subtraction for division he placed divisor below dividend and represented multiplication by abbreviations.

Brahmagupta was equally a past master in the field of shapes sizes and volumes. In the *Brahmasphutasiddhanta,* he gave remarkable formulae for the area of a cyclic quadrilateral and for the lengths of the diagonals in terms of the sides. He developed formulae and concepts to measure area and exact area of cyclic quadrilateral

His other discoveries include the value of pi and methods of measuring length, breath volume\and depth.

Although he made so many mathematical discoveries his sine tables based on the trigonometrical longitudes of planets aid a lot in modern gigantic calculations and calculations in the field of astronomy. What Galileo and Newton felt at later stages about earth's shape and gravity Brahamgupta had discovered hundreds of years ago.

In addition to the *Brahmasphutasiddhanta,* Brahmagupta wrote a second work on mathematics and astronomy which is the *Khandakhadyaka* written in 665 when he was 67 years old.

He died three years later in 668. Zero was not the brainchild of Western world but the product of Brahmagupta, the great Indian mathematician.

25

Robert Brown
(1773-1858)

Robert Brown is best known for his description of the natural continuous motion that is named after him. In addition, he recognised the fundamental distinction between the conifers and their allies (gymnosperms) and the flowering plants (angiosperms), recognised and named the nucleus as a constant constituent of living cells in most plants, and improved the natural classification of plants by establishing and defining new families and genera.

Brown was born in Montrose, Scotland on 21 December 1773. He studied at Marischal College in Aberdeen, and then medicine at the University of Edinburgh in 1775.

He joined the Fencibles regiment of the army as a surgeon in 1795. In December 1800 he accepted an offer of the position of naturalist on board the *Investigator* under Matthew Flinders, which was about to depart on its historic voyage to chart the coast of Australia. The *Investigator* arrived in King George Sound in what is now Western Australia in December 1801. For three and a half years Brown did intensive botanic research in Australia, collecting about 3400 species, of which about 2000 were previously unknown. A large part of this collection was lost, however, when the *Porpoise* was wrecked en route to England.

Rather than use Linnaeus's artificial classification, he followed Antoine de Jussieu's more natural system, adding his own modifications and using microscopic characters to help delimit species. By 1810 he had described 2,200 species, over 1,700 of which were new (including 140 new genera). He intended to produce an extensive treatise on Australian plants but the poor sales of the first volume, which appeared in 1810, led him to discontinue publication of the remainder.

In the course of his painstaking work Brown became very familiar with plant morphology, which led him to make many important observations. He found that in conifers and related plants the ovary around the ovule is missing, thus establishing the basic difference between these plants and flowering plants or between the gymnosperms and the angiosperms, as the two groups of seed-bearing plants were later named. He also observed and named the nucleus, recognizing it as an essential part of living cells.

From 1806 to 1822 Brown was librarian of the Linnean Society; in 1810 he also became librarian and curator at Banks's Soho Square residence. Banks stipulated in his will that on his death he should take charge of his house, library and herbarium. In 1820 he duly inherited this responsibility and in 1827 he donated Banks's library and herbarium to the British Museum on the understanding that the trustees established an independent botany department in the museum. Thus a botanical collection became accessible to the general public for the first time in Britain.

In 1827, while examining a suspension of pollen grains in water, under a microscope, Brown observed that the grains were in continuous erratic motion. Initially he believed that this movement was caused by some life force in the pollen, but when he extended his observations to inanimate particles suspended in water he found the same effect. This phenomenon was named Brownian motion and remained unexplained until the kinetic theory was developed.

He discovered that if particles were of a certain size (or smaller), the movement continued to occur. Brown observed the same movement in glass and rock particles, and theorised that the movement was not limited to living matter. The botanist concluded that the movement was caused by some phenomenon of physics and named the phenomenon 'Brownian motion'.

Brown continued his work in botanical research, focusing especially on work with a microscope. He led the field on research that studied fossils under the microscope, and was particularly interested in studying pollination among the higher plant species. His microscopic research led him to discover the nucleus of the cell (1831), which he observed in plant tissue and which he named cell nucleus.

In 1905, Albert Einstein suggested that Brownian motion was the result of the particles colliding with molecules. Nobel Prize winner, Jean Perrin, proved that Einstein's thesis of Brownian motion was correct. Brown's discovery provided the first evidence that proved the existence of atoms. The phenomenon of Brownian motion also led scientists to quantify Avagadro's number — a physical constant for describing random motion.

Brown was elected a fellow of the Royal Society in 1810 and became a Fellow of the Linnean Society in 1822. He was the President of the Linnean Society from 1849 to 1853.

He died on June 10, 1858 in London.

◆◆◆

26

Robert Wilhelm Eberhard Bunsen

(1811-1899)

Robert Wilhelm Eberhard Bunsen was a German chemist and physicist. He perfected the burner that was named after him, invented by British chemist/physicist Michael Faraday, and worked on emission spectroscopy of heated elements. He developed the spectroscope and discovered cesium and rubidium. He invented the gas burner and the photometer.

After attending school in Holzminden, Robert Bunsen studied chemistry at the University of Göttingen. He gained his doctorate at the age of 19 at the university in his native city of Göttingen with a thesis on hygrometers and then, from 1830 to 1833, travelled across western Europe.

After his return to Germany, Bunsen became a lecturer at Göttingen and began experimental studies of the (in)solubility of metal salts of arsenious acid. Today, his discovery of the use of iron oxide hydrate as a precipitating agent is still the best known antidote against arsenic poisoning.

In 1836, Bunsen succeeded Wöhler at Kassel. After teaching there for two years, he accepted a position at the University of Marburg, where he studied cacodyl derivatives.

In the 1840s, being keenly interested in geology, he proved experimentally how geysers work.

Bunsen was an extraordinary experimentalist and popular university teacher who made a name for himself in the 1830s with experiments using organic arsenic compounds. Although his work brought him quick and wide acclaim, he almost killed himself from arsenic poisoning. It also cost him the sight of one eye, when an explosion propelled a glass sliver into his eye.

In 1841, he created a carbon electrode that could be used instead of the expensive platinum electrode used in Grove's battery.

He taught for many years at the University of Marsburg (1838-51), but is most closely associated with the University of Heidelberg, where he worked from 1852 until his retirement in 1889. He invented many lab tools, including a grease-spot photometer, a galvanic battery and an ice calorimeter.

Bunsen was a great experimentalist, an expert in gas analysis and glass blowing, and a pioneer of photochemistry and spectroscopy. He also worked in electrochemistry, devising an improved version of the Grove cell. At Heidelberg he used his new cell to produce metals by electrodeposition.

In 1852, Bunsen took the position of Leopold Gmelin at Heidelberg. Using nitric acid, he was able to produce pure metals such as chromium, magnesium, aluminium, manganese, sodium, barium, calcium and lithium by electrolysis. A ten-year collaboration with Sir Henry Enfield Roscoe began in 1852, studying the formation of hydrogen chloride from hydrogen and chlorine.

In 1859, Bunsen discontinued his work with Roscoe and joined Gustav Kirchhoff to study emission spectroscopy of heated elements.

With Gustav Kirchhoff, in about 1859, he observed that each element emits a light of characteristic wavelength. These studies opened the field of spectrum analysis, which became of great importance in the study of the sun and stars.

In 1860 Robert Bunsen and Gustav Kirchhoff discovered two alkali metals, cesium and rubidium, with the aid of the spectroscope they had invented the year before. These discoveries inaugurated a new era in the means used to find new elements. The first 50 elements discovered—beyond those known since ancient times—were either the products of chemical reactions or were released by electrolysis. From 1860 the search was on for trace elements detectable only with the help of specialized instruments like the spectroscope.

The famous Bunsen burner was introduced by him in 1855, although a similar burner, used by Michael Faraday, did exist before Bunsen and the regulating collar was a later refinement. It was later named the 'Bunsen burner'. He greatly refined gas analysis and wrote a standard treatise on the subject, *Gasometrische Methoden* (1857, *Methods in Gas Measurement*).

When Bunsen retired at the age of 78, he shifted his interest to geology, which had long been a hobby of his.

He died in 1899.

27

Marie Curie

(1867-1934)

Marie Curie was a Polish-French physical chemist known for discovering radium, which is used to treat some diseases. She won the Nobel Prize for chemistry in 1911. She and her husband, Pierre Curie, also won the Nobel Prize for physics in 1903 for their work in radiation. The discovery of these elements laid the foundation for future discoveries in nuclear physics and chemistry.

Marie Curie, née Maria Sklodowska, was born in Warsaw on November 7, 1867. She received a general education in local schools and some scientific training from her father.

In 1891, she went to Paris to continue her studies at the Sorbonne where she obtained Licenciateships in Physics and the Mathematical Sciences. She later joined with the Faculty of Sciences at the Sorbonne. This made her the first woman to teach at the university level in France.

Under Russian control, Polish women could not attend college. Marie's sister, Bronya, went to Paris to study and later helped Marie with her education. Despite a limited knowledge of French, Marie succeeded with honours at the Sorbonne, where she graduated with degrees both in mathematics and chemistry. It was still very difficult, as a woman, for Marie to find work.

She met Pierre Curie, Professor in the School of Physics, in 1894 and in the following year they were married. She succeeded her husband as Head of the Physics Laboratory at the Sorbonne, gained her Doctor of Science degree in 1903.

Marie's legacy to science is that she correctly speculated that the radiation spontaneously released from the ore was nuclear rather than atomic.

The discovery of radioactivity by Henri Becquerel in 1896 inspired the Curies in their brilliant researches and analyses which led to the isolation of polonium, named after the country of Marie's birth, and radium.

In 1903, the Curies and Henri Becquerel received the Nobel Prize for physics for their work on radioactivity, and Marie was granted her doctorate the same year. She developed methods for the separation of radium from radioactive residues in sufficient quantities to allow for its characterization and the careful study of its properties, therapeutic properties in particular.

On April 19, 1906, following the tragic death of Pierre Curie, she took his place as Professor of General Physics in the Faculty of Sciences, the first time a woman had held this position. She was also appointed Director of the Curie Laboratory in the Radium Institute of the University of Paris, founded in 1914.

The importance of Mme. Curie's work is reflected in the numerous awards bestowed on her. Apart from the Nobel Prize for Physics in 1903 jointly with her husband, in 1911 she received a second Nobel Prize, this time in Chemistry, in recognition of her work in radioactivity. She also received, jointly with her husband, the Davy Medal of the Royal Society in 1903 and, in 1921, President Harding of the United States, on behalf of the women of America, presented her with one gram of radium in recognition of her service to science.

Marie founded the Radium Institute in Paris. Because the Curies had not patented the rights to radium, or the process to produce it, Marie had to make several trips to America to raise funds. Marie later had to cut back on her official duties, due to poor health. She died peacefully on July 4, 1934 in a nursing home.

◆◆◆

28

Sir James Chadwick

(1891-1974)

Sir James Chadwick was a British physicist who discovered in 1932 the particle in an atomic nucleus known as the neutron. His discovery formed the base for the investigation of the tougher questions of nuclear physics: the nature of the nucleus and its forces. In 1935, he received the Nobel Prize for Physics.

James Chadwick was born on October 20, 1891, in Cheshire, England. He was graduated from Manchester University's Honours School of Physics in 1911 and spent the next two years working on various radioactivity problems in the Physical Laboratory in Manchester, earning an M.Sc. degree in 1913 as well as the 1851 Exhibition Scholarship, which allowed him to continue his research and move to Berlin to work with Professor Hans Geiger. He remained to work with Ernest Rutherford.

In 1913, he received a scholarship to study in German, placing him in Germany at the beginning of World War I. After he was detained as a civilian prisoner of war, he returned to England in 1919 to carry out research at Cambridge University. In 1923, he became the assistant director of research at the Cavendish Laboratory.

Chadwick was elected Fellow of Gonville and Caius College and became assistant director of research in the Cavendish Laboratory in 1923. In 1927, he was elected a Fellow at the Royal Society.

He was awarded the Hughes Medal of the Royal Society in 1932.

Rutherford discovered that atoms have minute and dense nuclei, with the nucleus holding a positive charge in the charge of a hydrogen nucleus. Physicists wanted to determine where the extra mass was living. Chadwick helped answer this question when identifying the neutron (particle without an electric charge in the nucleus) in 1932. He proved the existence of neutrons, preparing the way towards the fission of Uranium 235 and the creation of the atomic bomb. He had created an experiment to answer the question of this unknown nucleus mass source.

Chadwick smashed alpha particles into beryllium, a rare metallic element, and allowed the radiation that was released to hit another target: paraffin wax. When the beryllium radiation hit hydrogen atoms in the wax, the atoms were sent into a detecting chamber. In physics it is known that only a particle having almost the same mass as a hydrogen atom could effect hydrogen in that manner. The experiment results showed a collision with beryllium atoms would release massive neutral particles, which he named neutrons. This provided the answer for hidden mass in atoms.

Chadwick's discovery advanced experimental work for all scientists. Since neutrons have no electrical charge, any neutron fired from a source has the ability to go through deep layers of materials and to go into the nuclei of the target atoms. After his work, scientists worldwide began bombardment of all types of materials with neutrons. It was discovered that when uranium is a target, nuclear fission becomes possible, resulting in nuclear weapons and nuclear power plants.

In 1935, Chadwick received the Nobel Prize for Physics for this discovery. In that same year, he was elected to the Lyon Jones Chair of Physics at the University of Liverpool.

From 1943 to 1946, Chadwick worked in the United States as Head of the British Mission collaborating with the Manhattan Project in Los Alamos and became a leading advocate for developing the atomic bomb in Britain, the predominant scientist associated with the effort. He worked with the British atomic bomb project, and was a science advisor to Oppenheimer on the Manhattan Project. The Manhattan Project was the first time an atomic bomb had been produced.

Apart from the Hughes Medal (Royal Society), he received the Copley Medal (1950) and the Franklin Medal of the Franklin Institute, Philadelphia (1951).

He returned to Cambridge in 1948, serving as Master of Gonville and Caius College until he retired in 1959. He acted as part-time member of the United Kingdom Atomic Energy Authority from 1957 to 1962.

Chadwick was knighted by King George VI in 1945, and he died in 1974 at Cambridge.

◆◆◆

29

Raymond Vahan Damadian

(1936)

Raymond Damadian invented the magnetic resonance imaging (MRI) scanner, which has revolutionised the field of diagnostic medicine. His MRI produced images of the interior of the body far more detailed than was possible with X-ray devices such as the CAT scanner. Since the device's approval in 1984 by the Food and Drug Administration hundreds have been put to use in medical institutions around the world.

Raymond V. Damadian was born in Forest Hills, New York in 1936. He studied violin at the Julliard School of Music in New York for eight years before winning a scholarship, at age 16, to the University of Wisconsin. There he received a B.S. in mathematics in 1956 and an M.D. degree from the Albert Einstein College of Medicine in New York in 1960.

Damadian later served as a fellow in nephrology at Washington University School of Medicine and as a fellow in biophysics at Harvard University, where he completed academic work in physics, physical chemistry and mathematics.

He studied physiological chemistry at the School of Aerospace Medicine in San Antonio, Texas.

After his internship, residency, and Fellowships at Washington University and Harvard, Damadian served for some time in the Air Force. He then joined the faculty of the State University of New York Downstate Medical Center in 1967. His training in medicine and physics led him to develop a new theory of the living cell, his Ion Exchanger Resin

Theory. His research into sodium and potassium in living cells led him to his first experiments with nuclear magnetic resonance (NMR) which caused him to first propose the MR body scanner in 1969.

Damadian spent the next years working with teams of graduate students to make his scanner a reality. Finally, in 1977, his team produced the first MRI scan of the human body, using a prototype device he called 'Indomitable' (now installed in the Smithsonian Institution).

He went on to collaborate with Wilson Greatbach, one early developer of the implantable pacemaker, to develop an MRI-compatible pacemaker.

Damadian founded the FONAR Corporation in 1978 for the manufacture of the MRI scanner which produced the first commercial scanner in 1980.

Later the company developed the first FDA-approved, first mobile, and first whole-body MR scanners. FONAR's patented Iron Circuit technology has enabled the company to develop seven different MRI products including the recently cleared-for-marketing FONAR 360°, a full-size room with two circular structures (the poles of the magnet) projecting from the ceiling and the floor. There are no obstructions between the patient and the walls of the scanner room, and the patient is accessible from any direction. Damadian is also working on the Stand-Up MRI, the only scanner that allows MRI patients to be scanned while standing up.

The Franklin Institute in Philadelphia gave its recognition of Damadian's work on MRI with the Bower Award in Business Leadership. He was also named Knights of Vartan 2003 'Man of the Year'.

He has earned the 2001 Lemelson-MIT Program's Lifetime Achievement Award, a National Medal of Technology (1988), and induction into the National Inventors Hall of Fame (1989). He continues to direct FONAR's scientific and financial progress, as Chairman and President.

◆◆◆

30

Sir Humphry Davy

(1778-1829)

Sir Humphry Davy was a British chemist best known for his experiments in electro-chemistry and his invention of a miner's safety lamp.

Humphry Davy was born on 17 December 1778 in Penzance in Cornwall.

After being educated in Truro, Davy was apprenticed to a Penzance surgeon. Here he evinced a great interest in chemistry and experimentation, using as his guide Lavoisier's famous work, Traité élémentaire de chimie. His obvious talents attracted the attention of Gregory Watt and Davies Giddy (later Gilbert), both of whom recommended him to Dr. Thomas Beddoes for the position of superintendent of the newly founded Pneumatic Institution in Bristol. He worked there from October 1799 to March 1801.

The Pneumatic Institution was investigating the idea that certain diseases might be cured by the inhalation of gases. Davy, sometimes perilously, inhaled many gases and found that the respiration of nitrous oxide produced surprising results. Inhalation of 'laughing gas'," as it was soon called, became a novel form of entertainment, although nearly 50 years passed before it was actually used as an anesthetic. Davy also experimented with the newly invented voltaic pile, or battery.

Davy published details of his research in his book *Researches, Chemical and Philosophical* (1799). This led to hia being appointed as a lecturer at the Royal Institution. He was a talented teache and his lectures attracted large audiences. Sir Joseph Banks and Count Rumford had founded the Royal Institution in 1799 as a research institute and as a place for educating young men in science and mechanics. Here Davy's genius emerged full-blown. Not only did his brilliant lectures attract a fashionable and intellectual audience, but he also continued his electrical research. He was a great success, with his lectures soon becoming a draw for fashionable London society. He became a fellow of the Royal Society in 1803 and was awarded its Copley Medal in 1805.

In 1806 he showed that there was a real connection between electrical and chemical behaviour; for this achievement Napoleon I awarded him a prize. In the same year he published *On Some Chemical Agencies of Electricity*.

In 1800, the Italian scientist Alessandro Volta had introduced the first battery. Davy used this for what is now called electrolysis. In 1807 he electrolysed molten potash and soda and announced the isolation of two new elements, naming them potassium and sodium. Metallic potassium emerged easily from molten potash and metallic sodium from lye. He discovered that the alkalis and alkaline earths are compound substances formed by oxygen united with metallic bases. He also studied the forces involved in these separations, inventing the new field of electrochemistry.

In 1808 he used electrolysis to discover and isolate calcium, barium, strontium, and magnesium. Later he showed that boron, aluminum, beryllium, and fluorine existed, although he was not able to isolate them. He also independently produced boron a few days after its first discoverers and was the first to recognise chlorine as an element.

Lavoisier had claimed that a substance was an acid because it contained oxygen. Davy doubted the validity of this claim and in 1810 showed that 'oxymuriatic acid gas' was not the oxide of an unknown element, murium, but a true element, which he named chlorine.

In 1812 Davy was knighted by the King George III for his great discoveries.

Napoleon I invited him to visit France, even though the two countries were at war. He and his wife went to France in 1813, taking with them as valet and chemical assistant the 22-year-old Michael Faraday. The French presented them with a curious substance isolated from seaweed, and Davy, working in his hotel room, was able to show that this was another new element, iodine.

When he returned to England, he was asked by a group of clergymen to study the problem of providing illumination in coal mines without exploding the methane there. In 1815, he received a letter from some Newcastle miners which told of the dangers they faced from methane gas. The gas often filled the mines, and could be sparked off by the candles they had in their helmets to light their work. The resulting fires and explosions caused many deaths. Davy separated the flame from the gas, and his 'Davy' lamp later became widely used. Davy gave the invention to the world without attempting to patent or otherwise exploit it. His invention of the miner's safety lamp in 1815 saved many lives and his electric arc lamp of 1809 was the start of electric lighting.

Working in another area, he demonstrated how electrochemical corrosion could be prevented.

One of Davy's most important contributions to history was that he encouraged manufacturers to take a scientific approach to production. His discoveries in chemistry helped to improve several industries including agriculture, mining and tanning.

Davy was made a baronet in 1818. In 1820, after Sir Joseph Banks had died, he was made president of the Royal Society. During the last of his years, he carried out studies in electromagnetism. He began the needed internal reform of the society, but bad health forced him to resign in 1827.

He died on May 29, 1829, in Geneva, Switzerland, where he was buried.

◆◆◆

31

Paul Adrien Maurice Dirac

(1902-1984)

Paul Dirac won the Nobel Prize in physics in 1933 for his discovery of anti-matter. Of the small group of young men who developed the complete theoretical formulation of quantum mechanics and revolutionised physics almost a century ago, he truly stands out.

Paul Adrien Maurice Dirac was born in Bristol, England, in 1902. His first degree, obtained at the Merchant Venturer's Technical College, was in electrical engineering, but he had no real interest in the subject.

After graduating he spent two years studying mathematics at the University of Bristol.

In 1923, at the age of 21, he left Bristol for Cambridge where he remained for most of his working life. At this time the world of physics was in turmoil. Experiments had shown that classical physicists could not explain the behaviour of atoms. The old principles of Isaac Newton didn't seem to apply to the microscopic world.

Dirac soon developed his own widely-acclaimed theory of quantum mechanics. His theory included wave mechanics, the version of quantum mechanics developed by Erwin Schrodinger, and matrix mechanics, the theory put forward by Werner Heisenberg.

At the time, it seemed miraculous. Albert Einstein described Dirac's theory as 'the most logically perfect of quantum mechanics'.

Perfect as it was, the theory was only a reformulation of a newly-discovered branch of physics. In 1928, Dirac made a breakthrough. He combined the theories of quantum mechanics and Einstein's special relativity. The resulting Dirac equation, still widely used today, was able to explain the mysterious magnetic and 'spin' properties of the electron. Like so many great discoveries, it required an extraordinary leap of imagination.

But there was a conundrum. The equation had two solutions, one representing the electron, the other representing its opposite, a particle with negative energy and positive charge that had never been seen or suspected before.

Dirac concluded that each electron had an 'anti-particle'. The two could be created or destroyed in matching pairs. He had predicted the existence of anti-matter, which makes up, at least in principle, half the universe. Heisenberg judged this to be the supreme achievement of 20th century physics.

A few months later, a Californian experimenter, Carl Anderson, discovered anti-matter for real, confirming Dirac's genius. The acts of creation and annihilation are now the mainstay of particle accelerators and high-energy physics.

For his achievement, Paul Dirac was awarded the Nobel Prize for Physics in 1933 at the age of 31.

From 1932 to 1969 Dirac held the Lucasian Chair of Mathematics in Cambridge, the post that Newton himself had once occupied. During this period he worked on a variety of topics including magnetic monopoles (hypothetical magnetic charges) and the speculation that the fundamental constants of physics might be gradually changing in a coordinated way.

After he retired from Cambridge in 1969, Paul Dirac moved to the United States where he became a professor of physics at Florida State University.

Dirac received many honours for his work. He refused to accept honorary degrees but he did accept honorary membership of academies and learned societies. The list of these is long but among them are USSR Academy of Sciences (1931), Indian Academy of Sciences (1939), Chinese Physical Society (1943), Royal Irish Academy (1944), Royal Society of Edinburgh (1946), Institut de France (1946), National Institute of Sciences of India (1947), American Physical Society (1948), National Academy of Sciences (1949), National Academy of Arts and Sciences (1950), Accademia delle Scienze di Torino (1951), Academia das Ciencias de Lisboa (1953), Pontifical Academy of Sciences, Vatican City (1958), Accademia Nazionale dei Lincei, Rome (1960), Royal Danish Academy of Sciences (1962), and Académie des Sciences Paris (1963). He was appointed to the Order of Merit in 1973.

He died in Tallahassee, Florida in 1984.

In November 1995 of a plaque was unveiled in Westminster Abbey commemorating Paul Dirac.

32

Gerhard Johannes Paul Domagk

(1895-1964)

German chemist and pathologist Gerhard Domagk researched infections caused by bacteria, and found that an industrial dye, prontosil rubrum, had antibacterial action that proved an effective treatment for staphylococci and haemolytic streptococci. For his discovery of prontosil's therapeutic effect, Dr Domagk was named a Nobel Prize winner in 1939.

Domagk was born in Lagow, Brandenburg (which is now Poland, but was then Germany) on October 30, 1895. Until he was fourteen he went to school in Sommerfeld, where his father was assistant headmaster. He himself was, from the age of 14, at school in Silesia until he reached the upper sixth form.

He then became a medical student at Kiel and, when the 1914-1918 War broke out, he served in the Army, and in December 1914 was wounded.

Later he was sent to join the Sanitary Service and served in, among other places, the cholera hospitals in Russia. During this time he was decisively impressed by the helplessness of the medical men of that time when they were faced with cholera, typhus, diarrhoeal infections and other infectious diseases. He was especially strongly influenced by the fact that surgery had little value in the treatment of these diseases and even amputations and other forms of radical treatment were often followed by severe bacterial infections, such as gas gangrene.

In 1918 he resumed his medical studies at Kiel and in 1921 he took his State Medical Examinations and graduated. He undertook laboratory work under Max Bürger on creatin and creatinin, and later metabolic studies and analysis under Professors Hoppe-Seyler and Emmerich.

In 1923 he moved to Greifswald and there became, in 1924, University Lecturer in Pathological Anatomy. His post-doctoral qualification was obtained that year at the Pathological Institute of the University of Greifswald.

In 1925 he held the same post in the University of Münster and in 1958 became professor of this subject.

During the years 1927-1929 he was, however, given leave of absence from the University of Münster to do research in the laboratories of the I.G. Farbenindustrie, at Wuppertal.

In 1929 a new research institute for pathological anatomy and bacteriology was built by the I.G. Farbenindustrie and there, in 1932, while searching for a way to combat bacterial infections by chemical means, Domagk stumbled upon the active substance dimethyl benzyl dodecyl ammonium chloride, which was later launched on the market as a 10 percent solution under the trade name Zephirol. Zephirol's intensive antibacterial effect and good skin compatibility quickly made the product an indispensable and universally applicable skin disinfectant that is still used today for disinfecting hands and instruments.

In that same year, Domagk made the discovery for which his name is so well known, the discovery that earned him the Nobel Prize in Physiology or Medicine for 1939, namely, the fact that a red dye-stuff, to which the name 'prontosil rubrum' was given, protected one against lethal doses of staphylococci and haemolytic streptococci. His work has thus given to medicine, and also to surgery, a whole new series of weapons that are effective against many infectious diseases.

The discovery of the antibacterial action of the sulphonamides was not, however, Domagk's only contribution to chemotherapy. He also discovered the therapeutic value of the quaternary ammonium bases and he also extended, in collaboration with Klarer and Mietzsch, his work on the sulphonamides.

Later, he attacked the problem of the chemotherapy of tuberculosis, developing for this the thiosemicarbazones (Conteben) and isonicotinic acid hydrazide (Neoteben). His work has undoubtedly resulted in more effective control of many infectious diseases which nowadays have lost the terrors they formerly caused. The supreme aim of chemotherapy is, in Domagk's opinion, the cure and control of carcinoma and he was convinced that this will be, in the future, achieved.

Domagk held honorary doctorates of the Universities of Bologna, Münster, Cordoba, Lima, Buenos Aires, and Giessen. He was made Knight of the Order of Merit in 1952, was awarded the Grand Cross of the Civil Order of Health of Spain in 1955. Other honours and distinctions bestowed upon him were: Paul Ehrlich Gold Medal and Paul Ehrlich Prize, University of Frankfurt (1956); Foreign Member of the British Academy of Science and of the Royal Society (1959); Honorary Member of the German Dermatological Society (1960); Japanese Order of Merit of the Rising Sun (1960).

Dr Domagk died on April 24, 1964.

◆◆◆

33

Thomas Alva Edison

(1847-1931)

Thomas Edison was probably the world's greatest inventor. He not only invented the first successful electric light bulb, but also set up the first electrical power distribution company. He invented the phonograph, and made improvements to the telegraph, telephone and motion picture technology. He also founded the first modern research laboratory. In addition to the electric light, he also invented a cement mixer, the automatic telegraph, and he improved Alexander Graham Bell's telephone.

Thomas Alva Edison was born on February 11, 1847 in Milan, Ohio, and grew up in Port Huron, Michigan. In his early life he was thought to have a learning disability and he could not read till he was twelve and later he himself admitted that he became deaf after an injury to his ears.

With only three months of formal education he became one of the greatest inventors and industrial leaders in history. Afterwards, he was taught at home. He was a very curious child.

He would experiment to try to find the answers.To make money for his experiments, he went to work at age 12 selling newspapers and candy on a train. When he had some spare time on the train, he would do experiments in the baggage car.

When he was 16 he went to work for the telegraph office sending messages.

When he was 22 years old he went to New York. He only had $1 in his pocket. He hunted for a job during the day, and at night he slept in the basement of a gold company. He watched everything around him very closely. Some equipment broke down and he was able to fix it because he had been watching it work before he went to sleep each night. The owners gave him a job. He improved the machine so much the company paid him $40,000 for his invention. He started the American Telegraph Works in New Jersey.

He built a laboratory in Menlo Park, New Jersey. It was here with his employees he made many of his inventions. He and his team worked to make a light bulb which would burn for a long time without burning out. They tried 1,500 materials and nothing worked well. Finally he tried a new material in the filament that burned nearly 200 hours.

After he had made the light bulb, he worked to make a power system so people could use the bulb. In 1882 he flipped a switch and 85 houses in New York City had electric lights for the first time.

In his lifetime, Edison patented 1,093 inventions, earning him the nickname 'The Wizard of Menlo Park'.

Edison invented the phonograph, a very helpful invention, but in 1868, while working as a telegrapher in Boston, he invented a vote recording machine. This was his first real invention, and he patented it in 1869.

Besides the light bulb, Edison developed the phonograph and the kinetoscope, a small box for viewing moving films.

He also improved upon the original design of the stock ticker, the telegraph, and Alexander Graham Bell's telephone.

Edison was also a good businessman. He not only designed important new devices, he created companies worldwide for the manufacture and sale of his inventions. He and Henry Ford became friends after he encouraged Ford to use the gasoline powered engine for the automobile.

In tribute to this important American, electric lights in the United States were dimmed for one minute on October 21, 1931, a few days after his death.

◆◆◆

34

Paul Ehrlich
(1854-1915)

Paul Ehrlich was undoubtedly one of the geniuses of his time. He could well be regarded as the father of haemoatology, immunology, chemotherapy and pharmacology, and is particularly remembered for the first effective cure for syphilis. He was the first to relate chemical structure with function successfully. He shared the 1908 Nobel Prize for physiology or medicine with Elya Mechnikov.

Paul Ehrlich was born into a comfortable, lively household in a country town in Prussian Silesia, about twenty miles south of Breslau, in 1854.

In 1860, when he was six years old, Ehrlich entered the local primary school. At age ten he went to the St. Maria Magdalena Humanistic Gymnasium in Breslau and boarded with a professor's family.

Ehrlich was educated at the Gymnasium at Breslau and subsequently at the Universities of Breslau, Strassburg, Freiburg-im-Breisgau and Leipzig.

After matriculating in 1872, Ehrlich took a disappointing introductory course in natural sciences at Breslau University and then spent three semesters at Strassburg, which largely determined his life's course.

Having passed the examination, he returned in 1874 to Breslau, where he completed studies for his medical degree, except for one semester in 1876 at the Physiology Institute of Freiburg im Breisgau and a final term at Leipzig in 1878.

In 1878 he obtained his doctorate of medicine by means of a dissertation on the theory and practice of staining animal tissues. This work was one of the results of his great interest in the aniline dyes discovered by W. H. Perkin in 1853.

Professor Frerichs, an imaginative clinician with deep interests in experimental pathology, encouraged Ehrlich's histological and biochemical researches, and the latter thereby gained lasting insights into diagnostic and therapeutic problems. Frerichs gave him every facility to continue his work with these dyes and the staining of tissues with them. Ehrlich showed that all the dyes used could be classified as being basic, acid or neutral and his work on the staining of granules in blood cells laid the foundations of future work on haematology and the staining of tissues. His reports on the morphology, physiology, and pathology of the blood cells advanced hematology into a new era by establishing methods of detecting and differentiating the leukaemias and anaemias.

In 1882 Ehrlich published his method of staining the tubercle bacillus that Koch had discovered and this method was the basis of the subsequent modifications introduced by Ziehl and Neelson, which are still used today. From it was also derived the Gram method of staining bacteria so much used by modern bacteriologists.

In 1882 Ehrlich became Titular Professor and in 1887 he qualified as a Privatdozent (honorary lecturer or instructor) in the Faculty of Medicine in the University of Berlin. Later he became an Associate Professor there and Senior House Physician to the Charité Hospital in Berlin.

In 1890 Robert Koch, Director of the newly established Institute for Infectious Diseases, appointed Ehrlich as one of his assistants, and Ehrlich then began the immunological studies with which his name will always be associated.

At the end of 1896 an Institute for the control of therapeutic sera was established at Steglitz in Berlin and Ehrlich was appointed its Director. Here he did further important work on immunology, especially on haemolysins. He also showed that the toxin-antitoxin reaction is, as chemical reactions are, accelerated by heat and retarded by cold and that the content of antitoxin in antitoxic sera varied so much for various reasons that it was necessary to establish a standard by which their antitoxin content could be exactly measured. This he accomplished with von Behring's antidiphtheritic serum and thus made it possible to standardise this serum in units related to a fixed and invariable standard. The methods of doing this that Ehrlich then established formed the basis of all future standardisation of sera. This work and his other immunological studies led Ehrlich to formulate his famous side-chain theory of immunity.

In 1897 Ehrlich was appointed Public Health Officer at Frankfurt-am-Main. Opened in 1899, the Royal Prussian Institute for Experimental Therapy was directed by him until his death sixteen years later. He also became Director of the Georg Speyerhaus, which was founded by Frau Franziska Speyer and was built next-door to Ehrlich's Institute.

These appointments marked the beginning of the third phase of Ehrlich's many and varied researches. He now devoted himself to chemotherapy, basing his work on the idea that the chemical constitution of drugs used must be studied in relation to their mode of action and their affinity for the cells of the organisms against which they were directed. To achieve this, Ehrlich tested, with the help of his assistants, hundreds of chemical substances selected from the even larger number of these that he had collected.

He studied, among other subjects, the treatment of trypanosomiasis and other protozoal diseases and produced trypan red, which was, as his Japanese assistant Shiga showed, effective against trypanosomes. He also established, with A. Bertheim, the correct structural formula of atoxyl, the efficiency of which against certain experimental trypanosomiases was known. This work opened a way of obtaining numerous new organic compounds with trivalent arsenic which he tested.

Subsequently, further work on this subject was done and eventually Ehrlich became famous as one of the main founders of chemotherapy.

Many honours came his way. After sharing the 1908 Nobel Prize with Metchnikoff, awarded in recognition of their work on immunity, he was renominated in 1912 and 1913 for his contributions to chemotherapy.

He received the Prussian Great Gold Medal of Science in 1903, the Liebig Medal in 1911, and the Cameron Prize in 1914. He was granted the title of Geheimer Obermedizinalrat in 1907 and of Wirklicher Geheimer Rat, with the predicate Excellenz, in 1911, from 1904 he was honorary ordinary professor at Göttingen, and in 1914 became ordinary professor at the new Frankfurt University. He held honorary or foreign memberships in about eighty scientific and medical societies.

Ehrlich died in 1915.

◆◆◆

35

Albert Einstein

(1879-1955)

Albert Einstein was a German-American physicist who developed a revolutionary theory about the relationships between time, space, matter and energy. He won a Nobel Prize in 1921. He is responsible for the special and general theory of relativity, and his work on the photoelectric effect. He also invented a few devices like Einstein calculator.

Albert Einstein was born at Ulm, in Württemberg, Germany, on March 14, 1879. Six weeks later the family moved to Munich, where he later on began his schooling at the Luitpold Gymnasium.

Later, they moved to Italy and Albert continued his education at Aarau, Switzerland and in 1896 he entered the Swiss Federal Polytechnic School in Zurich to be trained as a teacher in physics and mathematics.

In 1901, the year he gained his diploma, he acquired Swiss citizenship and, he accepted a position as technical assistant in the Swiss Patent Office. During his spare time, he produced much of his remarkable work and in 1908 he was appointed Privatdozent in Berne.

Einstein's first paper was quite revolutionary. In it, he examined an ever-present conflict in physics involving light.

Einstein regarded his second paper of 1905 as relatively unimportant. In it, he calculated a way of determining the size of molecules and found a value for Avogadro's number. By analysing diffusion rates of particles through liquids, he devised a simple model that facilitated his calculations. He submitted this paper for a Ph.D. thesis and he finally earned his Ph.D.

His third 1905 paper was more important. In it, Einstein pondered the interactions of particles in air and the related statistical consequences.

In Einstein's fourth 1905 paper, he introduced his revolutionary special theory of relativity and addressed this curiosity. He determined a formula using a simple coordinate transformation that quantifies time dilation. He showed that Maxwell's equations conform to relativity, and after mathematically verifying all of this, he concluded the revolutionary work.

More revolutionary work was to come. Einstein's next paper, published in 1907, showed that all mass consists of energy. Using his electromagnetic equations, he found that if a body releases E in energy, its mass decreases by E/c^2. He then finalised his theory that E = mc^2, showing that all matter possesses a proportionately large amount of energy.

In 1909 he became Professor Extraordinary at Zurich, in 1911 Professor of Theoretical Physics at Prague, returning to Zurich in the following year to fill a similar post.

In 1914 he was appointed Director of the Kaiser Wilhelm Physical Institute and Professor in the University of Berlin.

He became a German citizen in 1914 and remained in Berlin until 1933. Then he emigrated to America to take the position of Professor of Theoretical Physics at Princeton. He became a United States citizen in 1940 and retired from his post in 1945.

After World War II, Einstein was a leading figure in the World Government Movement, he was offered the Presidency of the State of Israel, which; he declined, and he collaborated with Dr. Chaim Weizmann in establishing the Hebrew University of Jerusalem.

Einstein fell ill, and on April 18, 1955, he died.

◆◆◆

36

Willem Einthoven

(1860-1927)

Willem Einthoven was a Dutch doctor and physiologist, who invented the first practical electrocardiogram also known as ECG. He was awarded the Nobel Prize for Physiology or Medicine in 1924.

Einthoven was born on May 21, 1860, in Semarang, Java (in what was then the Dutch East Indies and is now Indonesia). In 1866, his father died, and four years later, his mother moved the family to Utrecht, the Netherlands. There Willem Einthoven graduated from Hogere Burgerschool, and registered as a medical student at the University of Utrecht in 1878.

He received his Ph.D. degree in medicine in 1885. He then became professor of physiology at the University of Leiden. He remained at the university for the next 42 years. He later studied heart sounds, retinal currents, and acoustics. His laboratory at Leiden was a magnet for scientists from around the world.

As a student he was particularly influenced by the ophthalmologist Herman Snellen, and Franz Cornelis Donders. He worked as an assistant to Snellen in the renowned eye-hospital Gasthuis voor Ooglidders.

In January 1886 he qualified as a general practitioner.

He did important work on the function of bronchial muscles and in optics before turning his attention to improving A.D. Waller's electrocardiogram, which was unreliable and required complex mathematical corrections.

In 1887, the London physiologist Augustus Desiré Waller at St. Mary's Medical School, using a capillary electrometer, first succeeded in registering the current of the heart as deduced from the body surface. Étienne-Jules Marey in 1876 had recorded the first electrocardiogram using the mercury capillary electrometer, but Waller was the first to record the electrocardiogram of a human heart. Waller conducted his experiments on his bulldog Jimmie.

In 1889 Einthoven saw Waller demonstrate his technique at the First International Congress of Physiologists. Einthoven repeated this experiment and, in 1895, while working on the construction of this instrument and developing the necessary photographic equipment, with the capillary electrometer he registered graphic reproductions of the variations of the electric charges induced by the contractions of the heart's musculature, as well as heart sounds of humans and animals. He defined the physical constants of the capillary electrometer and calculated the true curve, which he called the electrocardiogram.

In about 1903, Einthoven invented a new instrument called the string galvanometer coated in silver based on ideas by Deprez and d'Arsonval who used a wire coil, and with it developed an improved method for measuring the electrical changes that take place in the body upon the contraction of the heart. While using his string galvanometer, he was able to detect and identify a number of different kinds of electrical waves associated with a beating heart. His machine could accurately measure and record the strength and rate of a patient's heartbeat. Eventually, he demonstrated that some of these waves result from contractions and electrical changes in the atria of the heart, and others from contractions and electrical changes in the ventricles.

Einthoven published the first electrocardiogram recorded on a string galvanometer in 1902. Then he published a description of his string galvanometer in 1909.

In 1905, Einthoven began transmitting electrocardiograms from the hospital to his laboratory 1.5 km away via telephone cable. On March 22 that year the first telecardiogram was recorded from a healthy and vigorous man and the tall R waves were attributed to his cycling from laboratory to hospital for the recording.

In 1912 Einthoven's research on the explanation of the respiratory changes in the electrocardiogram led him to the scheme of the equilateral triangle, considering the extremities as elongations of the electrodes. The information received from the contacts thus represents the projection of what takes place in the heart. With simultaneous registration of the three contacts, the size and direction of the resultant of all potential differences in the heart could be calculated minute by minute. Clinical electrocardiograms were studied by connecting patients with heart disease in the academic hospital to the instrument in Einthoven's laboratory by means of a cable.

His last major physical experiment, which he carried out in company with his son, was concerned with the reception of the radio telegrams broadcast by the machine transmitter 'Malabar' in Java. Einthoven and his son found the resonance point after they achieved a variation in tension of one micromicron, after which telegrams from the machine transmitter, working at top speed, were perfectly photographed on paper one centimetre wide.

Einthoven's last work was his treatise on the action current of the heart, which appeared posthumously in Albrecht Bethe's 1872 *Handbuch der normalen und pathologischen Anatomie*, Berlin 1925.

Einthoven received the 1924 Nobel Prize in physiology or medicine for his discovery of the mechanism of the electrocardiogram. After winning the award, he continued to work to perfect his string galvanometer throughout the rest of his career.

Einthoven was elected to foreign membership in the British Society in 1926.

He died on September 28, 1927, in Leiden.

37

Michael Faraday

(1791-1867)

Michael Faraday was a British chemist and physicist who contributed significantly to the study of electromagnetism and electrochemistry. Faraday is proclaimed as one of the greatest scientists in the world, and noted as a natural philosopher and the person who popularised science.

Michael Faraday was born in 1791 in Newington, England. He left school when he was 13. When he was 14, he became an apprentice to a bookbinder and bookseller. One of the books he found himself regularly binding was the *Encyclopedia Britannica.*

When he was twenty, Faraday began lecturing at the Royal Institution. His lectures were dramatic and enlightening. On one occasion he put water in iron containers and left them in the basement of the Institution to freeze. At the next lecture, the containers exploded before the audience and he had proven that water expands when frozen. He liquefied approximately 20 different gases, making refrigeration possible.

In 1812, Faraday attended four lectures given by the chemist Humphry Davy, a prominent scientist and experimentalist, who lectured at the Royal Institution of Great Britain. Faraday subsequently wrote to Davy asking for a job as his assistant. Davy turned him down but in 1813 appointed him to the job of chemical assistant at the Royal Institution. After six months, Faraday was doing chemical experiments and preparing explosive materials.

During the initial years of his scientific work, Faraday occupied himself mainly with chemical problems. He discovered two new chlorides of carbon and succeeded in liquefying chlorine and other gases. He isolated benzene in 1825, the year in which he was appointed director of the laboratory.

In 1827, Faraday succeeded Sir Davy as Chair of Chemistry at the Royal Institution and published the book, *Chemical Manipulation.* He later published *Experimental Researches in Electricity*, and *Experimental Researches in Chemistry and Physics.*

In 1831, experimental science was transformed when his experiments proved that frictional electricity from the clouds was the same as animal electricity, such as that of the electric eel. Faraday was the first scientist to recognise that a magnetic field could produce a current. His greatest achievement was the idea of the magnet and electric lines of force, causing a current to flow in the wire while the magnet is moving, which is called electromagnetic induction, based on 'Faraday's law of electrolysis'. This discovery was crucial in allowing electricity to be transformed from a curiosity into a powerful new technology. Faraday's discoveries of magnetic lines of force and electric lines of force were the impetus for the emergence of electronics, which has given us the television, telephone, fax machine and radio.

During the remainder of the decade he worked on developing his ideas about electricity. He was partly responsible for coining many familiar words including 'electrode', 'cathode' and 'ion'.

Faraday is also credited with the invention of a primitive electric motor. This motor was the first device that used an electric current to make an object move. The nature of industry and manufacture were changed by Faraday's laws of electrolysis. His experiments on the chemical effects of electric currents are the basis of electrochemistry.

Faraday's scientific knowledge was harnessed for practical use through various official appointments, including scientific adviser to Trinity House (1836-1865) and Professor of Chemistry at the Royal Military Academy in Woolwich (1830-1851).

Faraday's discovery (1845) that an intense magnetic field can rotate the plane of polarised light is known today as the Faraday effect. The phenomenon has been used to elucidate molecular structure and has yielded information about galactic magnetic fields.

He gave his name to the 'farad', originally describing a unit of electrical charge but later a unit of electrical capacitance.

However, in the early 1840s, Faraday's health began to deteriorate and he did less research.

In 1867, on 25 August, Faraday died in his home study at Hampton Court, where he had been given official lodgings in recognition of his contribution to science.

◆◆◆

38

Enrico Fermi

(1901-54)

Enrico Fermi was an Italian-born American physicist who was one of the chief architects of the nuclear age. He developed the mathematical statistics required to clarify a large class of subatomic phenomena, discovered neutron-induced radioactivity, and directed the first controlled chain reaction involving nuclear fission. He was awarded the 1938 Nobel Prize for Physics, and the Enrico Fermi Award of the U.S. Department of Energy is given in his honour.

Enrico Fermi was born in Rome, Italy, on September 29, 1901. He attended a local grammar school. His early aptitude for mathematics and physics was recognised and he decided to become a physicist.

In 1918, at the age of 17, he won a fellowship of the Scuola Normale Superiore to study at the University of Pisa from 1918 to 1922. He gained his doctor's degree in physics in 1922 at the age of 21.

Soon afterwards, in 1923, he was awarded a scholarship from the Italian Government After a short visit in Rome, Fermi left for Germany with a fellowship from the Italian Ministry of Public Instruction to study at the University of Gottingen under the physicist Max Born.

With a Rockefeller Fellowship, in 1924, he moved to Leyden to work with P. Ehrenfest, and later that same year he returned to Italy to occupy for two years the post of Lecturer in Mathematical Physics and Mechanics at the University of Florence.

In 1926 his paper on the behaviour of a perfect, hypothetical gas impressed the physics department of the University of Rome, which invited him to become a full professor of theoretical physics. Within a short time, Fermi brought together a new group of physicists, all of them in their early 20s. In 1926 he developed a statistical method, nowadays known as the 'Fermi statistics', for predicting the characteristics of electrons according to Pauli's exclusion principle (now referred to as 'fermions', which suggests that there cannot be more than one subatomic particle that can be described in the same way.

He became professor of theoretical physics at the University of Rome in 1927, a post which he retained until 1938.

The Royal Academy of Italy recognised his work in 1929 by electing him to membership as the youngest member in its distinguished ranks.

The theoretical work at the University of Rome was of first-rate importance, but new discoveries soon prompted Fermi to turn his attention to experimental physics. In 1932 the existence of an electrically neutral particle, called the neutron, was discovered by Sir James Chadwick at Cambridge University. In 1934 Frederic and Irene Joliot-Curie in France were the first to produce artificial radioactivity. Impressed by this work, Fermi conceived the idea of inducing artificial radioactivity by another method.

In 1934, he bombarded a variety of elements with neutrons. He discovered that slow moving neutrons were especially effective in producing radioactive atoms. Not realising he had split the atom, he announced what he thought were elements beyond uranium. His colleagues were inclined to believe that he had actually made a new, 'transuranic' element of atomic number 93. He was unaware that he was on the edge of a world-shaking discovery.

Fermi won the 1938 Nobel Prize for physics for his work on nuclear processes. He was given permission by the Fascist government of Mussolini to travel to Sweden to receive the award. As they had already secretly planned, he and his wife and family left Italy, never to return, for they had no respect for Fascism.

Fermi continued to conduct nuclear fission experiments at Columbia University. In 1940, his team confirmed that absorption of a neutron by a uranium nucleus can cause the nucleus to split into two nearly equal parts, releasing several neutrons and enormous amounts of energy.

Fermi was placed in charge of the Manhattan Project at the University of Chicago in 1942. He was assigned the task of producing a controlled, self-sustaining nuclear chain reaction. He designed the necessary apparatus, which he called an atomic pile, and on December 2, 1942, led the team of scientists who developed the first atomic pile and produced the first nuclear chain reaction. The project was moved to New Mexico in 1944. The testing of the first nuclear device, at Alamogordo Air Base in New Mexico on July 16, 1945, was followed by the dropping of atomic bombs on Hiroshima and Nagasaki a few weeks later.

After the war, Fermi continued his pioneering research on high energy particles. In 1946 he became Distinguished-Service Professor for Nuclear Studies at the University of Chicago and also received the Congressional Medal of Merit.

At the Metallurgical Laboratory of the University of Chicago, Fermi continued his studies of the basic properties of nuclear particles, with particular emphasis on mesons. He also was a consultant in the construction of the synchrocyclotron, a large particle accelerator at the University of Chicago.

In 1950 he was elected a foreign member of the Royal Society of London. In 1953, he visited Italy for the final time. Element number 100 was named for him, and the Enrico Fermi Award was established in his honour. He was the first recipient of this award of $25,000 in 1954.

On November 28, 1954, he died of cancer at the University of Chicago.

◆◆◆

39

Richard Phillip Feynman

(1918-1988)

Richard Feynman's main contribution was to quantum mechanics. He introduced Feynman diagrams that are graphic analogues of the mathematical expressions needed to describe the behaviour of systems of interacting particles. He was awarded the Nobel Prize in 1965, jointly with Schwinger and Tomonoga for fundamental work in quantum electrodynamics, with deep-ploughing consequences for the physics of elementary particles.

Richard Phillip Feynman was born on May 11, 1918, in Far Rockaway, a suburb of New York City. He lived there until 1935.

He studied at the Massachusetts Institute of Technology where he obtained his B.Sc. in 1939 and at Princeton University where he obtained his Ph.D. in 1942.

While at Princeton, Feynman worked on the Manhattan Project, which eventually led him to Los Alamos, New Mexico, in 1943 to work on the atomic bomb.

In 1946 he went to Cornell University, where he remained as an associate professor of theoretical physics until 1951.

He spent half of that year in Brazil lecturing at the University of Rio and then became a Tolman professor of physics at the California Institute of Technology, where he stayed for more than 30 years.

The significance of Feynman's contribution is enormous. He gave the theory of quantum electrodynamics a true physical meaning as well as an experimental use. The renormalised values for the electron's charge and mass provide finite, accurate means of measuring electron properties such as magnetic moment. This theory has also made a detailed description of the fine structure of the hydrogen atom possible. It also presents a precise picture of the collisions of electrons, positrons (anti-electrons), and photons in matter.

Feynman was awarded the Nobel Prize for his work in quantum electrodynamics in 1965, together with fellow American Julian Schwinger and Shinichiro Tomonaga of Japan, both of whom had separately developed similar theories, but using different mathematical methods. Feynman's theory was especially distinct from the other two in its use of graphic models to describe the intermediate states that a changing electrodynamic system passes through. These models are known as 'Feynman diagrams' and are widely used in the analysis of problems involving pair production, Compton scattering, and many other quantum-electrodynamic problems.

Feynman was fond of using visual techniques to solve problems. In addition to his Feynman diagrams, he developed a method of analyzing MASER (microwave amplification by stimulated emission of radiation) devices that relies heavily on creating accurate pictorial representations of the interactions involved. His method for analysing these devices greatly simplified and shortened the solutions, as well as brought out the important features of the device much more rapidly.

Feynman also worked on the theory of liquid helium, supporting the work of the Russian physicist L. D. Landau. Landau had shown that below a certain temperature the properties of liquid helium were similar to those of a mixture of two fluids; this is known as the two-fluid model. Feynman showed that a roton, which is a quantity of rotational motion that can be found in liquid helium, is the quantum mechanical equivalent of a rapidly spinning ring whose diameter is almost equal to the distance between the helium atoms in the liquid. This discovery gave Landau's theory a foundation in atomic theory.

Richard Feynman did work in many other areas of physics, including important work on the theory of Beta-decay, a process whereby the nucleus of a radioactive atom emits an electron, thereby transforming into a different atom with a different atomic number.

Feynman also contributed to a theory of partons, hypothetical hard particles inside the atom's nucleus, that helped produce the modern understanding of quarks. Quarks are the most elementary subatomic particles.

Feynman received many honours for his work. He was elected to the American Physical Society, the American Association for the Advancement of Science, the National Academy of Science, and the Royal Society of London. Among the awards he received were the Albert Einstein Award (1954), the Lawrence Award (1962), the Niels Bohr International Gold Medal (1973). He was a member of the National Academy of Science and a foreign member of the Royal Society in London.

Feynman was diagnosed with another cancerous abdominal tumor in October 1987 and died of complications on February 19, 1988.

◆◆◆

40

Benjamin Franklin

(1706-1790)

A noted polymath, Benjamin Franklin was a leading author and printer, satirist, political theorist, politician, scientist, inventor, civic activist, statesman and diplomat. He invented the lightning rod, bifocals, the Franklin stove, a carriage odometer, and the glass 'armonica'. He formed both the first public lending library in America and first fire department in Pennsylvania.

Benjamin Franklin was born on January 17, 1706 in Boston, Massachusetts.

Franklin's formal schooling ended early but his education never did. He read every book he could get his hands on. He taught himself simple algebra and geometry, navigation, logic, history, science, English grammar and a working knowledge of five other languages.

As young Benjamin loved to read he was apprenticed to his brother James, who was a printer. As an apprentice, he learned how to type and print. After helping James compose pamphlets and set type which was grueling work, 12-year-old Benjamin would sell their products in the streets.

At age 17, he ran away to Philadelphia to work on his own. He found a job as a printer and printed the *Philadelphia Gazette*, a newspaper. He invented the almanac in the print shop, selling about 10,000 copies a year.

In 1729, Benjamin Franklin bought a newspaper, the *Pennsylvania Gazette*. He not only printed the paper, but often contributed pieces to the paper under aliases. His newspaper soon became the most successful in the colonies. This newspaper, among other firsts, would print the first political cartoon, authored by Franklin himself.

But Franklin thrived on work. In 1733 he started publishing *Poor Richard's Almanac.* What distinguished his almanac were his witty aphorisms and lively writing. Many of the famous phrases associated with him, such as, "A penny saved is a penny earned" come from *Poor Richard.*

Franklin continued his civic contributions during the 1730s and 1740s. Among his chief accomplishments in this era was helping to launch the Library Company in 1731. During this time books were scarce and expensive. He recognised that by pooling together resources, members could afford to buy books from England. Thus was born the nation's first subscription library.

In 1743, he helped to launch the American Philosophical Society, the first learned society in America. Recognising that the city needed better help in treating the sick, he brought together a group who formed the Pennsylvania Hospital in 1751. The Library Company, Philosophical Society, and Pennsylvania Hospital are all in existence today.

By 1749 he retired from business and started concentrating on science, experiments, and inventions.

In 1743, he had already invented a heat-efficient stove — called the Franklin stove — to help warm houses efficiently. His invention of an iron furnace stove, called a Franklin stove, allowed people to warm their homes less dangerously and with less wood. As the stove was invented to help improve society, he refused to take out a patent.

Interestingly enough, Ben also established the first fire company and the first fire insurance company in order to help people live more safely. In 1736, he organided Philadelphia's Union Fire Company, the first in the city. His famous saying, "An ounce of prevention is worth a pound of cure," was actually fire-fighting advice.

Among Franklin's other inventions are swim fins, the glass armonica (a musical instrument) and bifocals. Ben had poor vision and needed glasses to read. He got tired of constantly taking them off and putting them back on, so he decided to figure out a way to make his glasses let him see both near and far. He had two pairs of spectacles cut in half and put half of each lens in a single frame. Today, we call them bifocals.

In the early 1750's he turned to the study of electricity. Franklin was very keen to show the world that lightning was electricity. In 1752, on a stormy day, he raised his kite with a key tied near his hand. He could feel the electric shock go through his body. He had finally proven and understood lightning/ electricity. Later that year, he invented the lightning rod which protected buildings and ships from lightning damage.

As postmaster, Franklin had to figure out routes for delivering the mail. He went out riding in his carriage to measure the routes and needed a way to keep track of the distance. He invented a simple odometer and attached it to his carriage.

In his old age, Ben retired from business and public service and wanted to spend his time reading and studying. He found, however, that his old age had made it difficult for him to reach books from the high shelves. Even though he had many grandchildren to help him, he invented a tool called a long arm to reach the high books. The long arm was a long wooden pole with a grasping claw at the end.

Now a man in his late seventies, Franklin returned to America. He became President of the Executive Council of Pennsylvania. He served as a delegate to the Constitutional Convention and signed the Constitution. One of his last public acts was writing an anti-slavery treatise in 1789.

Franklin died on April 17, 1790 at the age of 84.

◆◆◆

41

Galileo Galilei

(1564-1642)

Galileo is considered as one of the greatest contributors to the development of science. He was physicist, astronomer and philosopher, and his best known contributions lie in the development of telescope, first two laws of motion and also in astronomy. He is also considered as the father of astronomy, father of physics and father of science.

Galileo was born in Italy in 1564.Once he was old enough to be educated in a monastery, his parents sent him to the Camaldolese Monastery at Vallombrosa, southeast of Florence. He became a novice, intending to join the Order, but this did not please his father who had already decided that his eldest son should become a medical doctor. So Galileo returned to Florence.

He did continue his schooling in Florence, however, in a school run by the Camaldolese monks. In 1581 Vincenzo sent Galileo back to Pisa to enrol for a medical degree at the University of Pisa. The idea of a medical career never seems to have appealed to him. He attended courses in mathematics and natural philosophy. He returned to Florence for the summer vacations and there continued to study mathematics.

In the year 1582-83 Galileo was able to study the works of Euclid and Archimedes from the Italian translations.

Galileo began teaching mathematics, first privately in Florence and then during 1585-86 at Siena where he held a public appointment. During the summer of 1586 he taught at Vallombrosa, and in this year he wrote his first scientific book

The little balance La Balancitta which described Archimedes's method of finding the specific gravities (that is the relative densities) of substances using a balance.

In the following year he travelled to Rome to visit Clavius who was professor of mathematics at the Jesuit Collegio Romano there. He brought with him some results which he had discovered on this topic. After leaving Rome Galileo remained in contact with Clavius by correspondence and Guidobaldo del Monte was also a regular correspondent. Certainly the theorems which he had proved on the centres of gravity of solids, and left in Rome, were discussed in this correspondence. The correspondence began around 1588 and continued for many years.

Fantoni left the chair of mathematics at the University of Pisa in 1589 and Galileo was appointed to fill the post for him. He spent three years holding this post at the University of Pisa.

With strong recommendations from Guidobaldo del Monte, Galileo was appointed professor of mathematics at the University of Padua in 1592 at a salary of three times what he had received at Pisa.

On 7 December 1592 he gave his inaugural lecture and began a period of eighteen years at the university, years which he later described as the happiest of his life.

He returned to work on the theory of motion in 1602 and over the following two years, through his study of inclined planes and the pendulum, he formulated the correct law of falling bodies and had worked out that a projectile follows a parabolic path. However, these famous results would not be published for another 35 years.

In May 1609, Galileo received a letter from Paolo Sarpi telling him about a spyglass that a Dutchman had shown in Venice. From these reports, and using his own technical skills as a mathematician and as a craftsman, he began to make a series of telescopes whose optical performance was much better than that of the Dutch instrument. His first telescope was made from available lenses and gave a magnification of about four times.

To improve on this Galileo learned how to grind and polish his own lenses and by August 1609 he had an instrument with a magnification of around eight or nine. He immediately saw the commercial and military applications of his telescope for ships at sea. By the end of 1609 he had turned his telescope on the night sky and began to make remarkable discoveries.

The astronomical discoveries he made with his telescopes were described in a short book called the *Starry Messenger* published in Venice in May 1610. This work caused a sensation. Galileo claimed to have seen mountains on the Moon, to have proved the Milky Way was made up of tiny stars, and to have seen four small bodies orbiting Jupiter. These last, with an eye to getting a position in Florence, he quickly named 'the Medicean stars'.

In June 1610, Galileo resigned his post at Padua and became Chief Mathematician at the University of Pisa (without any teaching duties) and 'Mathematician and Philosopher' to the Grand Duke of Tuscany.

Galileo first turned his telescope on Saturn on 25 July 1610 and it appeared as three bodies (his telescope was not good enough to show the rings but made them appear as lobes on either side of the planet). Continued observations were puzzling indeed to him as the bodies on either side of Saturn vanished when the ring system was edge on. Also in 1610 he discovered that, when seen in the telescope, the planet Venus showed phases like those of the Moon, and therefore must orbit the Sun, not the Earth.

Other observations made by Galileo included the observation of sunspots. However by now his health was became poor and so even though he began to write his famous *Dialogue* in 1624 it took him six years to complete the work. During that time, he built himself a geometrical compass, and invented the first thermometer.

Galileo died in early 1642.

42

Johannes Gutenberg

(1398-1468)

Johannes Gutenberg was a German goldsmith and inventor best known for the Gutenberg press. He is also accredited with printing the world's first book using movable type, the 42-line 'Gutenberg Bible'.

Gutenberg was born in Mainz, Germany in 1398.

Gutenberg had an early start. His father used to work at the Mainz Mint and Johann usually went with him, he learned tips from jewellers and goldsmiths about how to carve or how to make metal. He stayed in Strasbourg for twenty years.

Gutenberg started his invention by making metal letters. He arranged them into a sentence and pressed a piece of paper against the letters with his hands. When he did it with his hands the ink did not come out evenly.

One day he watched people make paper out of animal skins. They had a press so that the water would dry out of the paper. That is when Johann decided he needed to make a press. He and his partners gathered the materials and started their work.

In 1438, Gutenberg began a business arrangement with Andreas Dritzehn, who funded his experiments in printing.

By 1450 he ran out of money for his paper, metal, and all the ink. He began a second arrangement with German businessman Johannes Fust. Fust lent him the money to start a printing business and build a large Gutenberg Press.

The Gutenberg press with its wooden and later metal movable type printing brought down the price of printed materials and made such materials available for the masses. It remained the standard until the 20th century. It was there in 1440 that Gutenberg created his printing press, a hand press, in which ink was rolled over the raised surfaces of moveable hand-set block letters held within a wooden form and the form was then pressed against a sheet of paper. The inventor's method of printing from movable type, including the use of metal moulds and alloys, a special press, and oil-based inks, allowed for the first time the mass production of printed books.

He worked on the *Catholicon of Johanns de Janua*, an enormous encyclopaedia.

On September 30, 1452, Gutenberg's *Bible* was published becoming the first book to be published in volume. *The Bible*, printed at Mainz, probably required several years of work; it began in 1452 and was completed not later than 1455 and printed in an edition of about 200 copies. It was of 42 lines, the oldest surviving book in the western world. While he was alive no printed material was credited to him. His *Bible* pages were not only edged with 22 carat gold but the inside front and back covers are adorned with a floral strip of antique gold. The text of the *Bible* is Latin. Coloured initials and other illuminations were hand drawn after the pages were printed. In design and workmanship, the *Gutenberg Bible* holds its place as one of the finest of all printed books.

The very first pages Gutenberg printed had only 40 lines per column. He realised these original pages were included in the very first issue of the *Gutenberg Bible*.

Gutenberg died in the year of 1468 in a fire when enemy troops attacked Mainz. He was buried in the town Franciscan church.

◆◆◆

43

William Harvey

(1578-1657)

William Harvey was an English physician who was the first to describe accurately how blood was pumped around the body by the heart.

William Harvey was born in Folkestone, Kent on 1 April 1578.

Harvey was educated at King's College, Canterbury and then at Cambridge University. He then studied medicine at the University of Padua in Italy, where the scientist and surgeon Hieronymus Fabricius tutored him. He graduated with honours in 1602 and returned to England where he earned yet another medical degree from Cambridge University. He then settled down to begin practising medicine.

Fabricius, who was fascinated by anatomy, recognised that the veins in the human body had one-way valves, but was puzzled as to their function. It was Harvey who took the foundation of Fabricius's teaching, and went on to solve the riddle of what part the valves played in the circulation of blood through the body.

On his return from Italy in 1602, Harvey established himself as a physician. In 1607, he became a fellow of the Royal College of Physicians and, in 1609, was appointed physician to St Bartholomew's Hospital. In 1618, he became physician to Elizabeth's successor James I and to James' son Charles when he became king. Both James and Charles took a close interest in and encouraged Harvey's research.

Harvey's research was furthered through the dissection of animals. He first revealed his findings at the College of Physicians in 1616, and in 1628 he published his theories in a book entitled *An Anatomical Study of the Motion of the Heart and of the Blood in Animals,* where he explained how the heart propelled the blood in a circular course through the body. His discovery was received with great interest in England, although it was greeted with some scepticism on the Continent.

A second ground-breaking book published by Harvey in 1651, *Essays on the Generation of Animals,* is considered the basis for modern embryology.

Harvey was also the first to suggest that humans and other mammals reproduced via the fertilisation of an egg by sperm. It took a further two centuries before a mammalian egg was finally observed, but nonetheless his theory won credibility during his lifetime.

Despite the uproar over each of Harvey's unconventional anatomical theories, he was recognised as a medical leader in his day. He was appointed doctor of physic at Oxford. Thanks to Charles I he was, for a short time, warden of Merton College, Oxford (1645 - 1646).

He died on 3 June 1657.

44

Stephen William Hawking

(1942-)

Stephen Hawking is a British physicist and leading authority on black holes—dense objects in space whose gravity is so strong that not even light can escape them. Hawking has also written best-selling books, including 'A Brief History of Time' and 'The Universe in a Nutshell'.

Stephen William Hawking was born on 8 January 1942 in Oxford, England. When he was eight, his family moved to St Albans, a town about 20 miles north of London. At eleven he went to St Albans School, and then on to University College, Oxford, his father's old college.

Hawking wanted to do mathematics, although his father would have preferred medicine. Mathematics was not available at University College, so he studied physics instead. After three years and not very much work he was awarded a first class honours degree in Natural Science.

Hawking then went on to Cambridge to do research in Cosmology, there being no one working in that area in Oxford at the time. After gaining his Ph.D. he became first a Research Fellow, and later on a Professorial Fellow at Gonville and Caius College.

After leaving the Institute of Astronomy in 1973 Hawking came to the Department of Applied Mathematics and Theoretical Physics, and since 1979 has held the post of Lucasian Professor of Mathematics.

Between 1965 and 1970 Hawking worked on singularities in the theory of general relativity devising new mathematical techniques to study this area of cosmology. Much of his work in this area was done in collaboration with Roger Penrose who, at that time, was at Birkbeck College, London.

From 1970 Hawking began to apply his previous ideas to the study of black holes. He worked on the basic laws which govern the universe.

With Roger Penrose he showed that Einstein's General Theory of Relativity implied space and time would have a beginning in the Big Bang and an end in black holes. These results indicated it was necessary to unify General Relativity with Quantum Theory, the other great scientific development of the first half of the 20th century. Continuing this work on black holes, Hawking discovered in 1970 a remarkable property. Using quantum theory and general relativity he was able to show that black holes can emit radiation and eventually evaporate and disappear.

Another remarkable achievement of Hawking's using these techniques was his no boundary proposal made in 1983 with Jim Hartle of Santa Barbara. The conjecture is that the universe has no edge or boundary in imaginary time, that both time and space are finite in extent, but they don't have any boundary or edge, there would be no singularities, and the laws of science would hold everywhere, including at the beginning of the universe. This would imply that the way the universe began was completely determined by the laws of science. His success with proving this made him work from that time on combining the theory of general relativity with quantum theory.

In 1971 Hawking investigated the creation of the Universe and predicted that, following the big bang, many objects as heavy as 109 tons but only the size of a proton would be created. These mini black holes have large gravitational attraction governed by general relativity, while the laws of quantum mechanics would apply to objects that small.

In 1982 Hawking decided to write a popular book on cosmology. By 1984 he had produced a first draft of *A Brief History of Time.* However he caught pneumonia and was rushed to hospital. The hospital in Geneva suggested to his wife that it was not worth keeping the life support machine on. But she was having none of that. He was flown back to Addenbrooke's Hospital in Cambridge, where a surgeon called Roger Grey carried out a tracheotomy. That operation saved his life but took away his voice.

Hawking was given a computer system to enable him to have an electronic voice. It was with these difficulties that he revised the draft of *A Brief History of Time* which was published in 1988. The book broke sales records in a way that it would have been hard to predict. By May 1995 it had been in *The Sunday Times* best-sellers list for 237 weeks breaking the previous record of 184 weeks. This feat is recorded in the 1998 *Guinness Book of Records.* Also recorded there is the fact that the paperback edition was published on 6 April 1995 and reached number one in the best sellers in 3 days. By April 1993 there had been 40 hardback editions of *A Brief History of Time* in the United States and 39 hardback editions in the UK.

Of course Hawking has received, and continues to receive, a large number of honours. He was elected a Fellow of the Royal Society in 1974, being one of its youngest fellows. He was awarded the CBE in 1982, and was made a Companion of Honour in 1989. He has also received many foreign awards and prizes and was elected a Member of the National Academy of Sciences of the United States.

◆◆◆

45

Werner Karl Heisenberg

(1901-1976)

German physicist Werner Karl Heisenberg was a pioneer in the formalisation of atomic theory. He won the 1932 Nobel Prize in physics for his discovery of the uncertainty principle, which states that it is impossible to specify the precise position and momentum of a particle at the same time. Heisenberg also developed the theory of matrix mechanics.

Werner Karl Heisenberg was born on December 5, 1901, in Würzburg, Germany. His high school years were interrupted by World War I, when he had to leave school to help harvest crops in Bavaria.

In 1920 he entered the University of Munich to pursue a degree in math. But the math professor wouldn't allow him into an advanced seminar, so he quit. He transferred to physics. He immediately took an interest in theoretical physicists, and soon met many scientists whose work would dominate the coming decades, including Niels Bohr, Wolfgang Pauli, Max Born, and Enrico Fermi.

One of his chief interests was working out problems involved in the Bohr-Rutherford model of the atom. He just barely received his Ph.D. in 1923 and became a professor at the University of Gottingen at age 22. He began working with Max Born in Gottingen.

Because he suffered from severe seasonal allergies, he left Bavaria for the island of Heligoland. While there he had time to think and work out problems with the atomic model. He realised the limitations of visual models and suggested working strictly with experimental data and mathematical results. To do this he applied a mathematical system to atomic physics, called matrix mechanics. It was a turning point for physics.

Many in the field disliked it because it didn't provide a physical model to relate to. Erwin Schrödinger came up with the theory of wave mechanics about a year later. Those uncomfortable with Heisenberg's system jumped on the wave mechanics side. The conflict between the theories was resolved when Schrödinger proved that they were, in fact, identical.

In 1926 Heisenberg joined Niels Bohr at the Institute for Theoretical Physics in Copenhagen. This turned out to be one of the most productive periods in Heisenberg's life.

In 1927 Heisenberg became professor of physics at Leipzig. He was puzzling over the basic quantum properties of electrons. He realised that the act of measuring an electron's properties by hitting it with gamma rays would alter the electron's behaviour. He tied this up in an equation using Planck's constant, and called it the uncertainty principle. While many resisted this idea, it eventually became accepted as a fundamental law of nature.

Later in 1927 Heisenberg returned to Germany and became the youngest full professor in the country. With the political turmoil in Germany and World War II, his life became complicated. There was a mass exodus of German scientists in the 1930s, but Heisenberg was one of the few top-notch scientists who decided to remain. Along with Max Planck, he expressed hope of being able to preserve Germany's scientific traditions and institutions.

But as the war began the government recognised, suspect or not, the importance of Heisenberg's knowledge. He was made director of the German Atom Bomb Project. He spent five years working on it.

Werner Heisenberg was the recipient, along with

Schroedinger and Paul Dirac, of the Nobel Prize for physics for 1932 for establishing the field of quantum mechanics.

At war's end, Heisenberg was captured by the Allies and was imprisoned in England for six months. He was released and returned to Germany where he re-established the Kaiser Wilhelm Institute for Physics, but renamed it the Max Planck Institute, in honour of his friend and colleague. He held many administrative posts in West Germany and represented his country at international meetings.

In 1941 he took the chair of theoretical physics at the University of Berlin and the directorship of the Kaiser Wilhelm Institute for Physics.

A few years later he introduced a new quantum number called isotopic spin. Heisenberg continued to contribute to particle physics, introducing useful computational techniques in the 1950s.

He retired in 1970, and died in 1976.

◆◆◆

46

Sir Frederick William Herschel

(1738-1822)

Sir Frederick William Herschel was a German-born British astronomer and composer. The founder of modern stellar astronomy, his discovery of Uranus in 1781 was the first identification of a planet in modern times. He developed the theory of nebulas and the evolution of stars. He catalogued many binary stars and made important modifications to the reflecting telescope. He also demonstrated that the solar system moves through space and he discovered infrared radiation.

Friedrich Wilhelm Herschel, better known as Sir William Herschel, was born in Hanover, Germany on November 15, 1738.

Music was an important part of his upbringing, and, at the age of fourteen, started out as an oboist in the Hanoverian Guards band and, as such, made a visit to England. Taking a position as an organist and music teacher at Bath, Herschel was to make England his home.

He rented a small reflecting telescope, but this only whetted his appetite to have his own, larger telescope. Since he didn't have enough money to buy one, he contrived to build it with the help of Alexander and Caroline. This eventually led to the construction of his largest telescope, a 48-inch reflector which he built with a 4,000 pound grant from King George III. However, most of his recorded observations were made with his 20-foot reflecting telescope. His systematic survey of the sky was one of the most important of his accomplishments.

In 1781 he communicated to the Royal Society the first of a series of papers on the rotation of the planets and of their several satellites. While engaged on them he noticed the curious appearance of a white spot near each of the poles of the planet Mars. On investigating the inclination of its axis to the plane of its orbit, and finding that it differed little from that of the earth, he concluded that its changes of climate also would resemble our own, and that these white patches were probably polar snow. He also discovered that, as far as his observations extended, the times of the rotations of the various satellites round their axes conform to the analogy of our moon by equalling the times of their revolution around their primaries.

On March 13, 1781, while scanning the skies with a 7-inch reflecting telescope, he observed an unusual object; it presented an extended disk-like shape. Herschel thought he had discovered a comet. He continued his observations, and calculations for months, discovering the orbit lay well beyond the orbit of Saturn and was fairly circular. Herschel's Comet was in fact a planet. Different names were suggested, including his own name, Herschel. He, however, wanted to call the new planet Georgium Sidus, after his new patron, George III. This name, however, did not find favour with the astronomical community. It was eventually named Uranus after the mythological god of the skies.

Herschel was granted a pension of 200 pounds a year and knighted by King George III, who also made him 'King's Astronomer'. Receiving a pension enabled Herschel to devote full time to astronomy.

Herschel's observations and discoveries are numerous. He observed sunspots and confirmed the gaseous nature of the sun. He discovered not only the planet Uranus, but two of its moons, and also two of Jupiter's moons.

His principal works were on stars. Two discoveries of primary importance is the movement of the solar system through space and the evidence that binary stars move around a common center of gravity. He discovered nearly 1,000 double stars.

In a long series of remarkable papers, addressed as usual to the Royal Society, and extending from the year 1784 to 1818, when he was eighty years of age, he demonstrated the fact that our sun is a star situated not far from the bifurcation of the Milky Way, and that all the stars visible to us lie more or less in clusters scattered throughout a comparatively thin, but immensely extended stratum. In 1785 he brought out the disc theory of the stellar system, anticipating the shape of our own galaxy. He believed that all nebulae are clusters of stars which he called island nebulae.

Herschel saw at the first view, in a grandeur not witnessed before, the Saturnian system with six satellites, five of which had been discovered long before by Christiaan Huygens and Giovanni Domenico Cassini, while the sixth, subsequently named Enceladus, he had, two years before, sighted by glimpses in his exquisite little telescope of 6-1/2 inch aperture, but now saw in unmistakable brightness with the towering giant he had just completed. On the 17th of September he discovered a seventh, which proved to be the nearest to the globe of Saturn. It has since received the name of Mimas. It is somewhat remarkable that, notwithstanding his long and repeated scrutinies of this planet, the eighth satellite, Hyperion, and the crape ring should have escaped him.

He also discovered the infrared range of sunlight.

The prince regent conferred a Hanoverian knighthood upon him in 1816. But a far more valued and less tardy distinction was the Copley medal assigned to him by his associates in the Royal Society in 1781.

Sir William Herschel died in Slough, England on August 25, 1822.

◆◆◆

47

Gustav Ludwig Hertz

(1887-1975)

German scientist Gustav Hertz achieved fame and success early in life when he and James Franck documented the changes in energy that occur when an electron strikes an atom. For their work Hertz and Franck received the Nobel Prize in Physics in 1925. Hertz was also involved in some of the Soviet Union's early research into atomic energy.

Hertz was born on July 27, 1887, in Hamburg, Germany. He first attended the Johanneum Realgymnasium in Hamburg, and after graduating in 1906 he began his college education at the University of Göttingen, majoring in mathematics and physics. He later transferred to the University of Münich and eventually ended up at the University of Berlin where he completed his education. During his studies he developed an interest in the field of experimental physics and ultimately finished his studies in this field.

In 1911, he graduated from the University of Berlin with a Ph.D.

In 1913 Hertz was offered the position of research assistant at the University of Berlin's Physical Institute. It was at this post that he first met Franck. Interested in the same questions of experimental physics, the two men decided to pursue their research collaboratively. The first assignment they resolved to concentrate on involved bombarding a metal surface with a stream of electrons and then studying the emission of electrons from the metal, thereby determining the effect the impact of electrons had on atoms. They were especially interested in the changes this bombardment would have on the atomic energy level.

Taking up experiments by German physicist Philipp E. A. von Lenard, and Albert Einstein on the photoelectric effect one step further, Hertz and Franck attempted to glean the make-up of electrons given off by a metal surface when it was bombarded by electrons instead of light.

The results of Hertz and Franck's experiments offered up one of the first pieces of experimental confirmation for Bohr's revolutionary new theory. This research demonstrated the quantitative relations between the series of spectra lines and the energy losses of electrons in collision with atoms corresponding to the stationary energy states of the atoms.

Shortly after his groundbreaking experiment was completed, Hertz was drafted into the German army; in 1914. He was gravely wounded in battle in 1915.

At the end of World War I Hertz moved back to Berlin where, in 1917, he was offered a position as a lecturer. In 1920 he was offered a position at the Philips Incandescent Lamp Works in Eindhoven, Netherlands. Where he stayed for five years. His new employment allowed him freedom to continue with his research work.

In 1925 Hertz and his family again returned to Germany, where he had been offered the position of professor of physics at the University of Hale. He also took over as the director of the Physical Institute at that university. In that same year, in recognition of his earlier work with Franck, the two men were jointly awarded the 1925 Nobel Prize for Physics for their work with atomic energy.

Hertz stayed at the University of Hale for three years before he once again moved back to Berlin. In 1928 he became a professor of physics at the Charlottenburg Technical University. He was also entrusted with the task of rebuilding the school's Physics Institute, a job that required much of his time. Still, he also continued his work in physics, and discovered a method of separating neon isotopes using a diffusion cascade.

Hertz was offered a position at the Siemens and Halske Company in Berlin in 1935. He remained at that position, continuing his research, throughout World War II.

In 1945 Hertz and his family moved to the Soviet Union. From 1945 tot 1954 he worked as the head of a research laboratory in the Soviet Union, when he was appointed Professor and Director of the Physics Institute at the Karl Marx University in Leipzig. He stayed in the Soviet Union, working on supersonics, radar, and continuing his research into atomic energy. Although he was seemingly hidden away, Hertz's work did not go unnoticed. In 1951 he won the Stalin Prize for his work on atomic energy. He stayed in the Soviet Union until he finished his term of employment in 1954.

After living briefly in East Germany, he was offered and accepted the position of director at the Karl Marx University's Physics Institute, located in Leipzig, Germany.

Hertz has published many papers, alone, with Franck, and with Kloppers, on the quantitative exchange of energy between electrons and atoms, and on the measurement of ionization potentials. He also is the author of some papers concerning the separation of isotopes.

In addition to receiving the Max Planck Medal from the German Physical Society, he was also named an honorary member of the Hungarian Academy of Sciences, a member of the Czechoslovakian Academy of Sciences, and was a foreign member of the Academy of Sciences of the USSR.

Hertz was a member of several prestigious scientific organisations, including the German Academy of Sciences in Berlin, and the Göttingen Academy of Sciences.

Hertz retired from Karl Marx University in 1961, at which time he was made professor emeritus. He returned for the last time to his former home in what still then was East Berlin.

He died there on October 30, 1975.

◆◆◆

48

Hipparchus

(160-125B.C.)

Hipparchus was a Greek astronomer who carried out his observations at Rhodes. He discovered the precession of the equinoxes and the eccentricity of the sun's path, determined the length of the solar year, estimated the distances of the sun and moon from the earth, drew up a catalogue of 1080 stars, fixed the geographical position of places by latitude and longitude, and invented trigonometry

Hipparchus was born in Nicaea in Bithynia, but spent much of his life in Rhodes. He is generally considered to be one of the most influential astronomers of antiquity, yet very little information available about him survives; his only extant work is his commentary on the astronomical poem of Aratus (third century B.C.), the *Commentary on the Phainomena of Eudoxus and Aratus.* Other works by him (now lost) included an astronomical calendar, books on optics and arithmetic, a treatise entitled *On Objects Carried Down by their Weight*, geographical and astrological writings, and a catalogue of his own work.

The *Almagest*, written by Ptolemy (second century A.D.) is the source of most of our knowledge about Hipparchus, who Ptolemy considered to be his most important predecessor. In his own astronomical work, Ptolemy made extensive use of the work of Hipparchus, building on the foundation laid by him.

Ptolemy described Hipparchus as 'industrious' and, repeatedly, as a great 'lover of truth'. That Hipparchus continued to be held in high regard is demonstrated by the various depictions of him on frontispieces of astronomical works published long after his death.

Hipparchus's many important and lasting contributions to astronomy included practical and well as theoretical innovations. He employed geometrical models, including the deferent-epicycle and eccentric previously used by Apollonius (flourished ca. 200 B.C.).

One of his contributions appears to have been the incorporation of numerical data based on observations into the geometrical models developed to account for the astronomical motions; Gerald Toomer has credited Hipparchus with the founding of trigonometry. Hipparchus was very interested in observation; his recorded observations span the years 147 to 127 BC. He used an instrument described by Ptolemy as a dioptra and may have invented the planispheric astrolabe. He made an early contribution to trigonometry producing a table of chords, an early example of a trigonometric table; indeed some historians go so far as to say that trigonometry was invented by him. He also introduced the division of a circle into 360 degrees into Greece.

Hipparchus made extensive observations of star positions, and is credited by some with the production of the first known catalogue of stars. He turned his attention to a wide variety of astronomical questions, including the length of the year, the determination of lunar distance and the computation of lunar and solar eclipses. He developed theories for the Sun and Moon demonstrating (as Ptolemy explained, Almagest, 421) 'that they are represented by uniform circular motions'.

Perhaps the discovery for which Hipparchus is most famous is the discovery of precession which is due to the slow change in direction of the axis of rotation of the earth. This work came from his attempts to calculate the length of the year with a high degree of accuracy.

Hipparchus's discussion of the motion of the points of solstice and equinox slowly from east to west against the background of the fixed stars is perhaps his most famous achievement; he has been therefore credited with the discovery of the precession of the equinoxes. Otto Neugebauer has suggested that Hipparchus, in fact, invented the theory of trepidation.

Perhaps most intriguing for historians of astronomy is Hipparchus's use of Babylonian astronomical material, including methods as well as observations. Many questions remain regarding the relationship between Babylonian and Greek astronomy, but his work provides a clear link. Toomer has argued that Hipparchus was responsible for the direct transmission of both Babylonian observations and procedures and for the successful synthesis of Babylonian and Greek astronomy.

Hipparchus was not only the founder of trigonometry but also the man who transformed Greek astronomy from a purely theoretical into a practical predictive science.

◆◆◆

49

Frederick Gowland Hopkins

(1861-1947)

The English biochemist Sir Frederick Gowland Hopkins discovered the amino acid tryptophan (1902, jointly with S. W. Cole), and later its essentiality; 'accessory food factors' (later named vitamins) 1906. For this work he shared with Christian Eijkman the 1929 Nobel Prize in Physiology or Medicine. He also discovered glutathione, and xanthine oxidase, the enzyme responsible for uric acid formation.

Frederick Gowland Hopkins was born on June 20, 1861, in Eastbourne, England. He was brought up by his widowed mother and an unmarried uncle who tended to ignore him. When he was seventeen, he was apprenticed as a chemist in a commercial laboratory, where for three years he performed routine analyses. At the same time, however, he also took part-time courses in chemistry at the University of London, eventually getting his degree.

An inheritance in 1881 allowed him to study chemistry at the Royal School of Mines and at University College, London. His work there brought him to the attention of Thomas Stevenson, who offered Hopkins the post of assistant in his laboratory at Guy's Hospital.

Feeling the need of more formal qualifications he began to work for a medical degree at Guy's in 1889. In 1894 he graduated from the University of London in both science and medicine and became an assistant in the department of physiology at Guy's Hospital. He joined the staff of Guy's Hospital and taught for several years.

Hopkins's first mature research paper concerned the chemistry of the pigments of butterflies' wings. His first work on this topic appeared in 1889, but his complete research was not published until 1896 in *Philosophical Transactions of the Royal Society* as 'Pigments of Pieridae'. He showed that the opaque white substance in the wings of this butterfly was uric acid - an example of the use of a normal excretory product for purposes of ornamentation. His research on butterfly pigments led him to extend his work to uric acid problems in humans.

In 1893 he published two papers describing a new method for determining uric acid in urine, which remained standard practice for many years. He published papers in 1898 and 1899 on the relation of uric acid excretion to diet, a reflection of the interest at that time in gout and its relation to uric acid formation.

In 1898, he was invited to teach physiology and anatomy at Cambridge University and it was at Cambridge—when Hopkins was well into his thirties—that his long, distinguished career really began. He served as professor of biochemistry (1914–43) but also established one of the great research institutions of the century.

In1901, working with S.W. Cole, a student at Cambridge, Hopkins discovered tryptophan, an important amino acid, and was able to isolate it from protein. A few years later, he demonstrated that tryptophan, and certain other amino acids, could not be manufactured in the body from other nutrients but had to be supplied as such in the diet. By so doing, he laid the foundation for the concept of the essential amino acid outlined by William Rose a generation later.

After his work with tryptophan, Hopkins' primary interest became the study of diet and its effect on metabolism. At the time, nutritional science was in a fairly primitive stage.

Hopkins had already noticed that his laboratory rats failed to grow on a diet of artificial nutrients, but grew rapidly when he added tiny amounts of cow's milk to their daily rations. He suspected, therefore, that normal food must contain substances missing from the pure fats, proteins and carbohydrates routinely used—for consistency—in nutritional studies. Terming these substances 'accessory food factors', he pointed out that they appeared to be necessary for growth. His two papers on the subject, in 1906 and 1912, are considered the first explanations of the concept of vitamins.

In 1907, Hopkins and Sir Walter Fletcher conducted pioneering research in another area of biochemistry when they demonstrated that working muscles accumulate lactic acid. And in 1922, he isolated the tripeptide (triple-linked) enzyme, glutathione, from living tissue and demonstrated its importance to the utilization of oxygen by tissue cells.

In 1910 Trinity College granted him a fellowship and appointed him praelector in physiological chemistry, a position with no formal obligations other than his own research.

For his pioneering work in vitamin research, Hopkins received the 1929 Nobel Prize in medicine or physiology (sharing the prize with Christiaan Eijkman).

He was knighted in 1925 and received numerous other awards, including the Royal Medal of the Royal Society of London in 1918 and the Copley Medal in 1926.

Hopkins was the recipient of many honorary degrees, honors, and prizes, including fellowship in the Royal Society (1906), knighthood (1925), the Copley Medal (1926), and the Nobel Prize in physiology or medicine (1929).

During his last few years, Hopkins suffered from a number of increasing disabilities, including loss of sight.

He died at Cambridge on May 16, 1947.

◆◆◆

50

Edwin Powell Hubble

(1889-1953)

Edwin Powell Hubble was an American astronomer. He demonstrated the existence of other galaxies besides the Milky Way. He also discovered that the degree of redshift observed in light coming from a galaxy increased in proportion to the distance of that galaxy from the Milky Way. This became known as Hubble's law, and would help establish that the universe is expanding.

Edwin Powell Hubble was born in the small town of Marshfield, Missouri, USA, on November 29, 1889.

In 1898, his family moved to Chicago, where he attended high school. He majored in science as an undergraduate at the University of Chicago. He went to Oxford University on a Rhodes scholarship, where he did not continue his studies in astronomy, but instead studied law.

On his return to America, he took a position as a high school Spanish teacher.

In 1913, Hubble returned from England and was admitted to the bar, setting up a small practice in Louisville Kentucky; but it didn't take long for Hubble to realise that his real passion was astronomy. After a year, he signed on as a graduate student at Yerkes Observatory in Wisconsin and embarked on the work that would one day make him famous: studying faint, hazy blobs of light called nebulae that are visible through even a modest telescope, and in 1917, he received a doctorate in astronomy from the University of Chicago.

Following a tour of duty in the first World War, Hubble took a job at the Mount Wilson Observatory in California, where he took many photographs of Cepheid variables through the 100-inch reflecting Hooker telescope, proving they were outside our galaxy, and determining the existence of several other galaxies such as our own Milky Way, which had until then been believed to be the universe.

In 1924, he announced the discovery of a Cepheid, or variable star, in a hazy patch of the sky called the Andromeda Nebula. He noticed that it contained stars resembling stars in the Milky Way but much fainter. He concluded that the stars in the Nebula must be much farther from Earth than stars in our own galaxy. His work proved that the Andromeda Nebula was actually a distant galaxy separate from our own.

At the time, most of his colleagues believed the Milky Way galaxy, a swirling collection of stars a few hundred thousand light-years across, made up the entire cosmos. But peering deep into space from the chilly summit of Mount Wilson, in Southern California, Hubble realised that the Milky Way is just one of millions of galaxies that dot an incomparably larger setting.

Hubble had also devised a classification system for the various galaxies he observed, sorting them by content, distance, shape, and brightness; it was then he noticed red shifts in the emission of light from the galaxies, seeing saw that they were moving away from each other at a rate constant to the distance between them. From these observations, he was able to formulate Hubble's Law in 1929, helping astronomers determine the age of the universe, and proving that the universe was expanding.

Hubble later studied the speed at which galaxies move away from each other. In 1929, he discovered that the farther apart galaxies are from each other, the faster they move away from each other. Based on this observation, Hubble concluded that the universe expands uniformly.

Hubble's observations that the universe was expanding outwards gave birth to the Big Bang Theory. He discovered the cosmos, and in doing so founded the science of cosmology.

Edwin Hubble left Mount Wilson in 1942, determined to help fight the Nazis in World War II; at first he wanted to join the armed forces as he had done during the First World War, but he realised he could do more for his country by offering his services as a scientist. In 1946, he was awarded the Medal of Merit, for exceptional conduct in providing outstanding services to citizens.

This was not the last of the honours bestowed upon Hubble, as in 1948, he was also elected Honorary Fellow of Queen's College, Oxford, for his notable contributions to Astronomy.

After the war ended, Hubble resumed his work at Mount Wilson. He was instrumental in the design of the Hale Telescope, which was set up at the Mount Palomar Observatory. He had the honour of being the first to use it.

The Hubble Space Telescope, launched by the National Aeronautics and Space Administration in 1990, was named in his honour.

Edwin Powell Hubble continued his work at both the Mount Wilson and Mount Palomar observatories until his death from a cerebral thrombosis.

He died on September 28, 1953.

◆◆◆

51

Christiaan Huygens

(1629-1693)

Christiaan Huygens was a Dutch physicist and mathematician who patented the first pendulum clock, which greatly increased the accuracy of time measurement. He laid the foundations of mechanics and also worked on astronomy and probability. In 1655, he discovered the ring and fourth satellite of Saturn. Huygens had a particular interest in the nature of light and was to propound a theory that it was undulating, thus striking upon the 'wave theory'.

Christiaan Huygens was born at The Hague on April 14, 1629. Tutored at home by private teachers until he was 16 years old, he learned geometry, how to make mechanical models and social skills such as playing the lute. His mathematical education was clearly influenced by Descartes who was an occasional visitor at the Huygens's home and took a great interest in the mathematical progress of the young Christiaan.

Huygens studied law and mathematics at the University of Leiden from 1645 until 1647. From 1647 until 1649 he continued to study law and mathematics but now at the College of Orange at Breda.

Huygens's first publications in 1651 and 1654 considered mathematical problems. Huygens soon turned his attention to lens grinding and telescope construction. Around 1654 he devised a new and better way of grinding and polishing lenses. Using one of his own lenses, Huygens detected, in 1655, the first moon of Saturn.

However others had different theories including Roberval and Boulliau. Boulliau had failed to detect Saturn's moon Titan, so Huygens realised that he was using an inferior telescope. By 1656 Huygens was able to confirm his ring theory to Boulliau and the results were reported to the Paris group. In *Systema Saturnium* (1659), he explained the phases and changes in the shape of the ring.

The following year he discovered the true shape of the rings of Saturn. Some, including the Jesuit Fabri, attacked not only Huygens theories but also his observations. However by 1665 even Fabri was persuaded to accept Huygens's ring theory as improving telescopes confirmed his observations.

In this same year he made his first visit to Paris. He informed the mathematicians in Paris including Boulliau of his discovery and in turn Huygens learnt of the work on probability carried out in a correspondence between Pascal and Fermat. On his return to Holland he wrote a small work *De Ratiociniis in Ludo Aleae* on the calculus of probabilities, the first printed work on the subject.

Huygens's work on the collision of elastic bodies showed the error of Descartes's laws of impact and his memoir on the topic was sent to the Royal Society in 1668. The Royal Society had posed a question on impact and Huygens proved by experiment that the momentum in a fixed direction before the collision of two bodies is equal to the momentum in that direction after the collision. Wallis and Wren also answered this question.

Circular motion was a topic which Huygens took up at this time but he also continued to think about Descartes's theory of gravity based on vortices.

Work in astronomy required accurate timekeeping and this prompted Huygens to tackle this problem. In 1656 he patented the first pendulum clock, which greatly increased the accuracy of time measurement. His work on the pendulum was related to other mathematical work which he had been doing on the cycloid as a result of the challenge by Pascal. He believed that a pendulum swinging in a large arc would be more useful at sea and he invented the cycloidal pendulum with this in mind. He built several pendulum clocks to determine longitude at sea and they underwent sea trials in 1662 and again in 1686. In the *Horologium Oscillatorium sive de motu pendulorum* (1673) he described the theory of pendulum motion. He also derived the law of centrifugal force for uniform circular motion. As a result of this Huygens, Hooke, Halley and Wren formulated the inverse-square law of gravitational attraction.

In 1661 Huygens visited London, particularly to find out more about the newly forming Royal Society meeting at that time in Gresham College. He showed his telescopes to the English scientists and they proved superior to those in use in England. The Duke and Duchess of York came to observe the Moon and Saturn through his telescope. While in London he saw Boyle's vacuum pump and he was impressed.

After his return to The Hague he carried out a number of Boyle's experiments for himself. He was elected to the Royal Society of London in 1663.

Huygens died in the same town that he was born in, The Hague, on July 8, 1695.

52

Jan Ingenhousz

(1730-1799)

The Dutch physician, chemist and engineer, Jan Ingenhousz is noted for his demonstration of the process of photosynthesis in plants. He was among the first to inoculate against smallpox; unlike the safer method later developed by Edward Jenner, however, Ingenhousz used live smallpox viruses.

Jan Ingenhousz was born on December 8, 1730, in Breda, Netherlands.

He studied medicine at the University of Louvain and graduated in 1752. After spending some years in several European capitals, he settled in London in 1779 and worked with the celebrated naturalist John Hunter.

While working at a London hospital, Ingenhousz became an expert in the technique of preventing smallpox by inoculation. Treatment at that time used a hazardous live virus instead of today's safer vaccine. In 1768, he travelled to Vienna, Austria, to inoculate Austria's royal family. His treatment was so successful that he was appointed court physician and awarded a lifetime income, which he used to finance independent research.

In 1779 Ingenhousz published his important book, *Experiments upon Vegetables - Discovering Their Great Power of Purifying the Common Air in the Sunshine and of Injuring It in the Shade and at Night*. In this work he anticipated by two years Joseph Priestley's discovery of the principles of photosynthesis, the process by which plants exude oxygen and absorb carbon dioxide, thus purifying the air for animals and man.

Ingenhousz was preoccupied by the problem of the fundamental balance in the animal and vegetable kingdoms, and this led him to investigate the mutual interdependence of plants and animals. He introduced the concept that the leaves of plants are great laboratories for cleansing and purifying the air. He also noted that oxygen is emitted by the underside of the leaves and that this is a daylight process, whereas in darkness even plants emit small quantities of carbon dioxide instead of absorbing it.

Inspired by Joseph Priestley's research on oxygen, Ingenhousz learned that only the green parts of plants can revitalise air that has been depleted of oxygen, and they do so only in the presence of sunlight. This was the first indication of light's role in plant life. He also discovered that only the visible light of the sun, not its heat, is necessary for photosynthesis. His research additionally proved that respiration occurs in all parts of the plant, including its roots and flowers. He later discovered that plants produce much more oxygen than they use, and, subsequently, that animal and plant life are naturally balanced in a system of mutual support.

Ingenhousz also broke new ground in physics and chemistry. He improved phosphorus matches, invented a hydrogen-fueled lighter, and mixed an explosive propellant for firing pistols. He also invented an improved apparatus for generating large amounts of static electricity (1766) and made the first quantitative measurements of heat conduction in metal rods (1789).

Ingenhousz built electrical machines and invented the plate electric machine. He also wrote a two-volume treatise dealing with problems in. Ingenhousz also opposed the theory of subtle electrical fluids and repeated some of the experiments on plant electricity to disprove the accepted view that positive electricity was good for the growth of plants and that negative electricity retarded it.

Ingenhousz died in Wiltshire, England, on Sept. 7, 1799.

◆◆◆

53

Karl Guthe Jansky

(1905-1950)

Karl Guthe Jansky was an American physicist and radio engineer who, in 1932, discovered that the Milky Way galaxy emanates radio waves; he did not follow up his discovery, but it marked the birth of radio astronomy.

Karl Jansky was born in Norman, Oklahoma on October 22, 1905. He went to the local schools in Madison, Wisconsin and after high school, the University of Wisconsin.

Karl Jansky attended the University of Wisconsin where he majored in physics. He received his bachelors degree with honours in 1927. As a superb student, Jansky was elected to Phi Beta Kappa.

After completing his B.S., Jansky started studying for a masters degree at Wisconsin. He completed the coursework but not a masters thesis, so Jansky did not graduate with an MS degree. However in 1936, the University of Wisconsin counted his early papers on radio astronomy for the thesis requirement and Jansky finally earned his masters degree.

Jansky took a job at Bell Labs in 1928. He was initially assigned to the Cliffwood, New Jersey laboratory, but moved to the Holmdel, New Jersey laboratory after two years. He worked on minimising the noise in short-wave radio receivers, which Bell Telephone Company (forerunner of AT&T) used for telephone communications.

He was given the task of investigating factors that could interfere with radio waves used for long-distance communication. He designed a linear directional antenna, which, mounted on wheels from a Model T Ford, could scan the sky. It was mounted on a turntable that allowed it to rotate in any direction, earning it the name 'Jansky's merry-go-round'. By rotating the antenna, one could find what the direction was to any radio signal.

He identified all the sources of interference, such as thunderstorms, except for one weak emission. This he found to be unconnected with the Sun and in 1931 he discovered that the radio interference came from the stars.

Jansky built the necessary receivers and analysed the noise in detail. Some of the noise was from thunderstorms, but there was also a component to the radio noise that did not seem to be terrestrial in origin. He recognised that this component was celestial because the strength of the signal varied with Earth's rotation period. The radio waves were coming from the centre of the Milky Way galaxy.

After recording signals from all directions for several months, Jansky identified three types of static: nearby thunderstorms, distant thunderstorms, and a faint steady hiss of unknown origin. He spent over a year investigating the third type of static. It rose and fell once a day, leading him to think at first that he was seeing radiation from the Sun. But after a few months of following the signal, the brightest point moved away from the position of the Sun. The signal was repeated not every 24 hours, but every 23 hours and 56 minutes. This is a characteristic of the fixed stars and other objects far from our solar system (sidereal day). He eventually figured out that the radiation was coming from the Milky Way and was strongest in the direction of the centre of our Milky Way galaxy, in the constellation of Sagittarius.

The discovery was widely publicised, appearing in the *New York Times* of May 5, 1933.

Jansky wrote several scientific papers during the 1930s on his discovery of celestial radio waves. He published his findings in the *Proceedings of the Institute of Radio Engineers* in December

1932, the date that marks precisely the beginnings of radio astronomy. In his paper he made two astute comments: that the radio emission was somehow connected with the Milky Way and that it originated not from the stars but from interstellar ionised gas. He did not pursue his suggestions and it was left to Grote Reber, the amateur astronomer, to keep the subject alive until it developed into a major research field after 1945. These pioneering papers on radio astronomy make Jansky the father of radio astronomy.

Jansky's discovery was serendipitous. Not only was it by chance that he had chosen a frequency at which the galactic centre emits large amounts of radiation and at which the earth's atmosphere is transparent, he also was working at a period of minimum sunspot activity which occurs only every 11 years. At sunspot maximum, the ionosphere would have blocked all extraterrestrial radio waves at the 20 MHz frequency, and signals from the Milky Way would not have been detected.

The unit of radio-wave emission strength was named the jansky in his honour.

During World War II, Jansky, like most American scientists and engineers, worked full time on the war effort. Defence projects, such as the development of radar, had to take priority over radio astronomy.

After the war ended, Bell Labs started to work on using microwaves for telephone communication purposes, rather than the short radio waves that Jansky had been studying. He contributed to this microwave work, but his health was failing.

He died on February 14, 1950.

54

Edward Jenner

(1749-1823)

Edward Jenner was an English country doctor who pioneered vaccination and thus laid the foundation of modern concepts of immunology. His discovery in 1796 was an immense medical breakthrough and has saved countless lives. He was known as the father of immunology.

Edward Jenner was born on May 17 1749 in the small village of Berkeley in Gloucestershire.

At age eight his schooling began at Wooton-under-Edge and was continued in Cirencester. At 13 he was apprenticed to Daniel Ludlow, a surgeon, in Sodbury.

In 1770 Jenner went to London to study with the renowned surgeon, anatomist, and naturalist John Hunter, but never took any examinations to obtain a medical degree. Instead, he purchased a medical degree from a Scottish university and later applied for and was granted an M.D. degree from Oxford University. He returned to his native Berkeley in 1773.

Jenner had been interested in nature as a child, and this interest expanded under Hunter's guidance. He aided in Hunter's zoological studies in many ways during his few years in London and then from Berkeley.

In Eastern countries the practice of inoculation against smallpox with matter taken from a smallpox pustule was common. This practice was introduced into England in the early 18th century. Although such inoculation aided in the prevention of the dreaded and widespread disease, it was dangerous. When Jenner returned to Berkeley he continued his observations for many years until he was fully convinced that cowpox did, in fact, confer immunity to smallpox.

On May 14, 1796, he vaccinated a young boy with cowpox material taken from a pustule on the hand of a dairymaid who had contracted the disease from a cow. The boy suffered the usual mild symptoms of cowpox and quickly recovered. A few weeks later the boy was inoculated with smallpox matter and suffered no ill effects.

In 1798, after carrying out further successful tests, he published his findings. He submitted a paper to the Royal Society in 1797 describing his experiment but was told that his ideas were too revolutionary and that he needed more proof. Undaunted, he experimented on several other children, including his own 11-month-old son. In 1798 the results were finally published. His findings rank among the most important medical discoveries of all time.

Jenner found a great deal of scepticism to his ideas and was subject to much ridicule. A cartoon was drawn, showing cows coming out of various parts of people's bodies after they had been vaccinated with cowpox. However, he persevered and eventually, doctors found that vaccination did work and by 1800 most were using it.

Jenner was awarded £30 000 by Parliament to enable him to continue carrying out his tests. Deaths from smallpox plummeted and vaccination spread through Europe and North America.

Jenner was also an educated naturalist and horticulturist, an amateur geologist and zoologist (he was elected as a Fellow of the Royal Society for a paper on the nesting habits of the cuckoo) and a fossil hunter who discovered the bones of a plesiosaur in 1819.

Jenner died of a cerebral hemorrhage in Berkeley on January 26, 1823, aged 74.

55

James Prescott Joule

(1818-1889)

James Prescott Joule was a British physicist who, with German physicists, Hermann von Helmholtz and Julius von Mayer, discovered the law of the conservation of energy. In 1840, he stated a law, now called Joule's Law, that heat is produced in an electrical conductor. The International unit of energy, the joule, is named in his honour.

James Joule was born at Salford near Manchester on December 24, 1818. A rather frail boy, he received his early education at home.

His scientific researches began in his youth when he invented an electromagnetic engine. In 1839, in the laboratory in his home, he began his studies of electrical motor efficiency, which ultimately led to his development of the mechanical theory of heat. In connection with this work he became one of the first to realise the necessity for standard units in electricity and to advocate establishing them.

In the course of his efficiency experiments Joule made his first discovery - now known as Joule's law: the heating of a conductor depends upon its resistance and the square of the current passing through it. He presented this important generalisation in a paper before the Royal Society in London in 1840.

Joule's study of the interrelation of heat and electrical energy may have stimulated his study of the relationship between heat and mechanical work. His approach was direct: he used the mechanical energy provided by falling weights to heat water by stirring it and made precise measurements of the heat produced and the energy lost by these weights. The results provided the first value of the mechanical equivalent of heat, corresponding to a temperature increase of 1F of 1 pound of water for the expenditure of 838 foot-pounds of work. The apparent simplicity of his experiment is quite misleading, for enormous experimental skill, great care, and limitless patience were needed to get repeatable results; experts regard his work as demonstrating exceptional skill.

Joule presented the results of these mechanical work experiments in a paper, which he read at the meeting of the British Association in 1843, but no notice was taken of them. During the next six years, using variations in procedure, he continued his measurements and consistently substantiated his first results.

His reports continued to be overlooked until 1847, when they came to the attention of William Thomson (later Lord Kelvin). He realised their significance, and through his efforts Joule finally got an attentive hearing of his work in 1849, when his paper was accepted for publication by, the Royal Society. His only other notable work, done with Thomson, led to the discovery of the so-called Joule-Thomson effect in 1862.

Joule made valuable contributions to the fields of heat, electricity, and thermodynamics. His work established the mechanical theory of heat, and he was the first to determine the relationship between heat energy and mechanical energy

Joule discovered the first law of thermodynamics, which is a form of the law of conservation of energy.

In his honour, the value of the mechanical equivalent of heat is usually represented by the letter J, and a standard unit of work is called the joule.

Joule remained an isolated amateur scientist for most of his life. Beginning about 1872 his health deteriorated. He died at his home in Sale, Cheshire, on October 11, 1889.

◆◆◆

56

Heike Kommerlingh Onnes

(1888-1946)

Heike Kamerlingh Onnes was a Dutch experimental physicist distinguished for his work in the field of low-temperature physics. He was the first scientist to succeed in liquefying helium, a breakthrough which yielded a previously unattainable degree of cold. This accomplishment won him the 1913 Nobel Prize in physics, in addition to numerous other awards. He is also credited with the discovery of superconductivity.

Kamerlingh Onnes was born in Groningen, the Netherlands, on September 21, 1853.

He was initially educated at Groningen High School and in 1870 he enrolled in the physics programme at the University of Groningen. The following year he submitted an essay on vapour density and won first prize in a contest sponsored by the University of Utrecht.

In October 1871, he transferred to the University of Heidelberg in Germany, where he was taught by the eminent German chemist Robert Wilhelm Bunsen. He was one of only two students allowed to work in the private laboratory of German physicist Gustav Robert Kirchhoff.

In April 1873, he returned to the University of Groningen, where he spent the next five years studying for his doctorate. In 1878, he moved to Delft Polytechnic where he became an assistant to the professor of physics there.

In 1879 he was awarded his physics doctorate magna cum laude. At Delft Polytechnic, he composed a paper on the general theory of fluids from the perspective of kinetic theory. He soon realised though that such a general theory of the nature of fluids required accurate measurements of volume, pressure, and temperature over as wide a range of values as possible. To this end, he turned his attention to the problem of attaining and maintaining very low temperatures.

In 1882, at the age of twenty-nine, Kamerlingh Onnes accepted Holland's first chair in experimental physics at Leiden University. He also became the director of the laboratory there, where he was able to pursue his interest in low-temperature physics, also known as cryogenics. He spent the rest of his career at Leiden. During the next forty-two years, he established it as the undisputed world headquarters of low-temperature research.

When Kamerlingh Onnes began his pioneering work, cryogenic physics was a relatively unknown science. Before him, the liquefaction of gases at very low temperatures was considered an end in itself, but he was interested in low-temperature physics in order to gather experimental evidence about the atomic nature of matter.

He set out to cool gases such as oxygen, hydrogen, and helium to extremely low temperatures. His first objective was to liquefy oxygen. He vapourised oxygen, then liquefied it, and then forced it under pressure into a closed, circulating system. The system was bathed in gases that had achieved progressively lower temperatures than the circulating oxygen. This methodology proved successful and Kamerlingh Onnes was able to produce about fourteen litres of liquid air an hour.

In 1908, he finally succeeded in the long-elusive goal of liquefying helium. He now set out to solidify the liquid helium in order to reach even lower temperatures, and in 1910, by boiling liquid helium under reduced pressure, he reached just over one degree above absolute zero.

Kamerlingh Onnes used these temperatures to extend the range of his research into the properties of substances at low temperatures, and the results of these investigations were published regularly in English.

In 1911, Kamerlingh Onnes discovered superconductivity, the complete disappearance of electrical resistance in various metals at temperatures approaching absolute zero. He also discovered that the superconductor effect can be negated without changing the temperature by the application of a magnetic field.

Kamerlingh Onnes and his team remained preoccupied with the challenge of crystallising helium. In 1913 he was awarded the Nobel Prize for physics for his investigations into the properties of matter at low temperatures leading to the discovery of liquid helium.

By 1921, he came within a degree of reaching absolute zero, and for the next three years he relentlessly pursued his quest. In 1926, he came across further peculiarities in the behaviour of helium at 2.2 degrees Kelvin. This time he did not dismiss his findings as due to technical faults but began to seriously consider the possibility that some kind of fundamental change in helium occurred at this temperature. Unfortunately, he did not live long enough to resolve the mystery.

Kamerlingh Onnes was widely recognised for his work in low-temperature physics, and he received a number of awards in addition to the Nobel Prize. In 1904, he received the first of many distinctions when he was created Chevalier of the Order of the Netherlands Lion. In that same year, his students and colleagues at Leiden issued a *Gedenkboek*, a survey of the work carried out at the laboratory from 1882 to 1904. A second *Gedenkboek* was issued in 1922, commemorating Kamerlingh Onnes's forty-year tenure as professor of experimental physics at Leiden. In 1912, he was awarded the Royal Society of London's Rumford Medal, and four years later the society made him a foreign member. In 1923, he was elevated from Chevalier to Commander of the Netherlands Lion.

Kamerlingh Onnes died at Leiden on February 21, 1926.

◆◆◆

57

Lord William Thomson Kelvin

(1824-1907)

Lord Kelvin was a Scottish mathematician and physicist, noted for the early search carried out in static electricity and magnetic phenomena. His research in the transmission of electric current was to lead to the laying down of submarine cables, the ultimate one being that laid down on the floor of the Atlantic. It was for this work that he was knighted in 1866. He also discovered the Thomson effect in thermoelectricity. His work went beyond pure science; he built instruments for his workshop, such as the ampère-meter, the volt-meter and the watt-meter. He invented the reflecting galvanometer and the siphon recorder, an instrument by which telegraphic messages are recorded in ink fed from a siphon

William Thomson Kelvin was born on June 26, 1824 in Belfast Ireland.

He attended Glasgow University from the age of 10. This early age is not quite as unusual as one would think, for at that time the universities in Scotland to some extent competed with the schools for the most able junior pupils. He began what we would consider university level work in 1838 when he was 14 years old.

In the session 1838-39 he studied astronomy and chemistry. The following year he took physics which included a study of heat, electricity and magnetism. His *Essay on the Figure of the Earth* won him a gold medal from the University of Glasgow when he was 15 years old and it was a truly remarkable work containing important ideas which he returned to throughout his life.

In 1841 Thomson entered Cambridge and in the same year his first paper was published. A more important paper on the uniform motion of heat and its connection with the mathematical theory of electricity was published in 1842 while he was studying for the mathematical tripos examinations at Cambridge.

Thomson took the final part of the Mathematical Tripos examinations in 1845. He graduated with a BA. Further examinations saw him become first Smith's prizeman and he was elected a fellow of Peterhouse.

His interest in the French approach, and advice from his father, meant that after taking his degree Thomson went to Paris. There he worked in the physical laboratory of Henri-Victor Regnault and he was soon taking part in deep discussions with Biot, Cauchy, Liouville, Dumas, and Sturm. He began trying to bring together the ideas of Faraday, Coulomb and Poisson on electrical theory.

Thomson returned from Paris to Glasgow and, in 1846, was unanimously elected professor of natural philosophy at the University.

In 1847-49 he collaborated with Stokes on hydrodynamical studies, which Thomson applied to electrical and atomic theory. This collaboration with Stokes was to last for over fifty years with frequent letters on scientific matters being exchanged.

The thermodynamical studies of Thomson led him to propose an absolute scale of temperature in 1848. The absolute scale that he proposed was based on his studies of the theory of heat, in particular the theory proposed by Sadi Carnot and later developed by Clapeyron. The Kelvin absolute temperature scale, as it is now known, was precisely defined much later after conservation of energy had become better understood. It derives its name from the title, Baron Kelvin of Largs that Thomson received from the British government in 1892, and named after him because of his proposal in this 1848 paper.

In 1852 Thomson observed what is now called the Joule-Thomson effect, namely, the decrease in temperature of a gas when it expands in a vacuum. Joule's ideas on heat were to change Thomson's views over the years. The dynamical theory of heat led Thomson to also think of a dynamical theory for electricity and magnetism.

In 1856 he sent a paper on this subject to the Royal Society of London entitled *Dynamical illustrations of the magnetic and helicoidal rotary effects of transparent bodies on polarised light.* This work by him in 1856 on electricity and magnetism is important for it was these ideas which led Maxwell to develop his remarkable new theory of electromagnetism.

He introduced laboratory work into the degree courses, keeping this part of the work distinct from the mathematical side. He encouraged the best students by offering prizes.

Another of Thomson's famous pieces of work was his joint project with Tait to produce their famous text *Treatise on Natural Philosophy* which they began working on in the early 1860s. These were remarkable volumes which became the standard texts for many generations of scientists.

Thomson designed and implemented many new devices, including the mirror-galvanometer that was used in the first successful sustained telegraph transmissions in transatlantic submarine cable. He had joined a group of industrialists in the mid- 1850s on a project to lay a submarine cable between Ireland and Newfoundland. The cable was successfully laid in 1858.

For his work on the transatlantic cable Thomson was knighted in 1866 and made Baron Kelvin of Largs in 1892.

He was elected to the Royal Society in 1851, received its Royal Medal in 1856, received its Copley Medal in 1883 and served as its president from 1890 to 1895.

Kelvin died on December 17, 1907.

◆◆◆

58

Johannes Kepler

(1571-1630)

Johannes Kepler was a German mathematician and astronomer who discovered that the Earth and planets travel about the sun in elliptical orbits. He gave three fundamental laws of planetary motion. He also did important work in optics and geometry.

Kepler was born in the small town of Weil der Stadt in Swabia Württemburg, in the Holy Roman Empire of German Nationality, on December 27, 1571.

He was a sickly child but his evident intelligence earned him a scholarship to the University of Tübingen to study for the Lutheran ministry. There he was introduced to the ideas of Copernicus and delighted in them.

In 1596, while a mathematics teacher in Graz, he wrote the first outspoken defence of the Copernican system, the *Mysterium Cosmographicum*.

In 1612 Kepler moved on to Linz. In 1619 he published *Harmonices Mundi,* in which he describes his 'third law'.

In spite of more forced relocations, Kepler published the epitome *Astronomiae* in 1621. This was his most influential work and discussed all of heliocentric astronomy in a systematic way. He then went on to produce the Rudolphine Tables that Tycho had envisioned long ago. These included calculations using logarithms, which he developed, and provided perpetual tables for calculating planetary positions for any past or future date. He used the tables to predict a pair of transits by Mercury and Venus of the Sun, although he did not live to witness the events.

Kepler was the first to correctly explain planetary motion, thereby, becoming founder of celestial mechanics and the first 'natural laws' in the modern sense; being universal, verifiable, precise.

In his book *Astronomia Pars Optica,* for which he earned the title of founder of modern optics, he was the first to investigate the formation of pictures with a pin-hole camera: first to explain the process of vision by refraction within the eye: first to formulate eyeglass designing for nearsightedness and farsightedness: and First to explain the use of both eyes for depth perception.

In his book *Dioptrice* (a term coined by Kepler and still used today) he was the: first to describe real, virtual, upright and inverted images and magnification: first to explain the principles of how a telescope works: and first to discover and describe the properties of total internal reflection.

His book *Stereometrica Doliorum* formed the basis of integral calculus. He was the first to explain that the tides are caused by the Moon: tried to use stellar parallax caused by the Earth's orbit to measure the distance to the stars; the same principle as depth perception. Today this branch of research is called astrometry: He Was the first to suggest that the Sun rotates about its axis in *Astronomia Nova*: he was the first to derive the birth year of Christ, that is now universally accepted: he was the first to derive logarithms purely based on mathematics, independent of Napier's tables published in 1614: He coined the word 'satellite' in his pamphlet *Narratio de Observatis a se quatuor Iovis sattelitibus erronibus*

Thanks in part to a telescope he received from Galileo, Kepler also advanced the science of optics. His achievements in astronomy and mathematics shaped our current understanding of the solar system.

Johannes Kepler died in Regensburg in 1630.

◆◆◆

59

Gustav Robert Kirchhoff

(1824-1887)

Gustav Robert Kirchhoff was a German physicist who is remembered as one of the founders of the science of spectroscopy. He is also known for Kirchhoff's laws, formulated in 1845 while he was still a student, which refer to the currents and electromotive forces in electrical networks.

Gustav Kirchhoff was born in Königsberg, East Prussia, in 1824.

He went to University at the age of 18 to read math. He graduated from the Albertus University of Königsberg in 1847 where he attended the mathematico-physical seminar directed by Franz Ernst Neumann and Friedrich Julius Richelot and was influenced by the former. Kirchhoff was also a student of Gauss.

In the same year, he moved to Berlin, where he stayed until he received a professorship at Breslau.

His first published paper won him a prize, and a place on the Berlin Physicists Society. He published a paper on straight and circular conductors, and this formed his thesis.

In 1845 Kirchhoff first announced Kirchhoff's laws, which allow calculation of the currents, voltages, and resistances of electrical networks. He completed this study as a seminar exercise; it later became his doctoral dissertation. He proposed his law of thermal radiation in 1859, and gave a proof in 1861. He was called to the University of Heidelberg in 1854, where he collaborated in spectroscopic work with Robert Bunsen. Extending the theory of the German physicist Georg Simon Ohm, he generalised the equations describing current flow to the case of electrical conductors in three dimensions. In further studies he demonstrated that current flows through a conductor at the speed of light.

He was a physicist who made important contributions to the theory of circuits using topology and to elasticity. Kirchhoff's laws, finally announced in 1854, allow calculation of currents, voltages and resistances of electrical circuits extending the work of Ohm

In 1857, he worked on conduction in telegraph wires. He discovered that the velocity of transmission is the same as the speed of light.

Together Kirchhoff and Bunsen discovered caesium and rubidium in 1861.

At Heidelberg he ran a mathematico-physical seminar, modelled on Neumann's, with the mathematician Leo Koenigsberger.

In 1862 he was awarded the Rumford Medal for his researches on the fixed lines of the solar spectrum, and on the inversion of the bright lines in the spectra of artificial light.

In 1875 Kirchhoff accepted the first chair specifically dedicated to theoretical physics at Berlin.

Kirchhoffs law in thermodynamics was established in the town of Heidelberg in the Rhineland in 1386.

Kirchhoff's circuit rules named after him are two statements about multi-loop electric circuits that embody the laws of conservation of electric charge and energy and that are used to determine the value of the electric current in each branch of the circuit.

Kirchhoff died in 1887, and was buried in the St Matthäus Kirchhof Cemetery in Schöneberg, Berlin.

◆◆◆

60

Robert Koch

(1843-1910)

Robert Koch, a German Physician, is well known to the world of microbiology for his significant contributions, especially in the area of microbial techniques. He introduced analine dyes for staining bacteria; used agar-agar and gelatin to prepare solid culture media; stressed the need for pure culture to study microbes in details; confirmed germ theory of disease, and laid down Koch's postulates to test the pathogenesity of causative agents. He also discovered the casual organisms of anthrax disease of cattle (Bacillus anthracis) and tuberculosis (Mycobacterium tuberculosis).

Robert Koch was born on December 11, 1843, at Clausthal, in what is now Germany, in the Upper Harz Mountains.

At the age of five he taught himself to read, and attended the local high school, showing an interest in biology. He enrolled in medical classes at the University of Göttingen in 1862, and in 1866 he passed the qualifying examinations. He spent some time in clinical study in Berlin but did not wish to engage in general practice. When the Franco-Prussian War broke out in 1870, he was accepted for service in the army.

In 1872 Koch was appointed district medical officer at Wollstein. That year he began his bacteriological research with a microscope his wife gave him. His first achievement was to isolate and identify the anthrax bacillus (1876.) Following the publication of some of his early findings, he was appointed to the Imperial Health Office at Berlin in 1880.

In 1882 he isolated and identified the tubercle bacillus (*Mycobacterium tuberculosis*), and in 1883, while leading an expedition to Egypt and India, he identified the bacterium that causes cholera (*Vibrio cholerae*).

In 1885 Koch was appointed professor of hygiene and bacteriology at the University of Berlin. In 1891 the Institute for Infectious Diseases was founded for him, and he acted as director until 1904.

One of the first diseases Koch studied was anthrax, an ancient and highly fatal cattle disease. Koch, attracted by the frequency of occurrence and the unusual behaviour of anthrax, set out to solve the problem. He studied bacterial diseases not only in humans but also in animals, and identified, among others, the cause of rinderpest, the lethal and economically important cattle plague of Africa.

In arriving at these conclusions, Koch acted on certain principles that are often referred to as 'Koch's postulates': to prove that an organism is the specific cause of any disease, it must be present invariably in all cases; it must be isolated in pure culture; and when a susceptible host is inoculated with a live culture, the disease must be reproduced. For the first time he irrefutably proved the manner in which anthrax arises and is transmitted. Thus the foundations of medical bacteriology were laid, and rational principles of hygiene and epidemiology in man and animals were established.

His work was facilitated by many of the techniques he and his associates developed to isolate bacteria and grow them on culture media in the laboratory. He published many papers and books and fostered the development of a whole generation of bacteriologists and medical scientists in other fields, not only in his native Germany but from many other nations as well.

With Jakob Henle he developed the Henle-Koch postulates, four basic criteria that are required for proof that a micro-organism caused a disease: (1) the organism can be isolated in every case of the disease; (2) it can be cultivated in pure culture;

(3) cultured organisms can induce the disease in experimental animals; and (4) the organism can be recovered from the infected experimental animals.

In 1881 Koch announced his discovery of the tubercle bacillus. He isolated the organisms from tubercular lesions and grew them successfully in pure cultures.

Another major discovery which revolutionised bacteriology was Koch's use of culture media which could be rendered solid, for example, blood serum by heating, meat broth by adding gelatin or agar, a product derived from seaweed. Thus it can be readily understood how within some 10 years a whole series of specific pathogens — including the causal agents of cholera, typhoid fever, and diphtheria; common pyogenic bacteria which cause suppuration in wounds; and varieties of intestinal flora— were isolated by Koch and others.

Robert Koch was awarded the Nobel Prize in medicine in 1905, a fitting capstone to his distinguished career.

He died in Baden-Baden on May 27, 1910.

◆◆◆

61

Karl Landsteiner

(1868-1943)

Karl Landsteiner was an Austrian-American pathologist, biologist and physician. He is noted for his development in 1901 of the modern system of classification of blood groups from his identification of the presence of agglutinins in the blood, and in 1930 he received the Nobel Prize in Physiology or Medicine. With Alexander S. Wiener, he identified the Rh factor in 1937. Landsteiner and Erwin Popper discovered the poliovirus in 1909.

Karl Landsteiner was born in Vienna on June 14, 1868.

In 1885, when he was seventeen, Landsteiner passed the entrance examination for medical school at the University of Vienna, where early in his training he expressed enthusiasm for the study of chemistry. He took a year off from school at the age of twenty for his obligatory military service.

Landsteiner graduated from medical school at the age of 23 and immediately began advanced studies in the field of organic chemistry, working in the research laboratory of his mentor, Ernst Ludwig In Ludwig's laboratory his interest in chemistry blossomed into a passion for approaching medical problems through a chemist's eye.

For the next ten years, he worked in a number of laboratories in Europe, studying under some of the most celebrated chemists of the day: Emil Fischer, a celebrated protein chemist who subsequently won the Nobel Prize for chemistry in 1902.

The nature of antibodies began to interest him while he was serving as an assistant to Max von Gruber in the Department of

Hygiene at the University of Vienna from 1896 to 1897. During this time he published his first article on the subject of bacteriology and serology, the study of blood. He had found a subject that was to occupy his entire scientific career.

Landsteiner moved to Vienna's Institute of Pathology in 1897, where he was hired to perform autopsies. He continued to study immunology and the mysteries of blood on his own time.

In 1900, Landsteiner wrote a paper in which he described the agglutination of blood that occurs when one person's blood is brought into contact with that of another. He suggested that the phenomenon was not a pathology, as was the prevalent thought at the time, but was due to the unique nature of the individual's blood. In 1901, he demonstrated that the blood serum of some people could clump the blood of others. From his observations he devised the idea of mutually incompatible blood groups. He placed blood types into three groups: A, B, and C (later referred to as O). Two of his colleagues subsequently added a fourth group, AB.

In 1907 the first successful transfusions were achieved by Dr. Reuben Ottenberg of Mt. Sinai Hospital, New York, guided by Landsteiner's work. Landsteiner's accomplishment saved many lives on the battlefields of World War I, where transfusion of compatible blood was first performed on a large scale.

In 1902 Landsteiner was appointed as a full member of the Imperial Society of Physicians in Vienna. That same year he presented a lecture, together with Max Richter of the Vienna University Institute of Forensic Medicine, in which the two reported a new method of typing dried blood stains to help solve crimes in which blood stains are left at the scene.

In 1908 he took charge of the department of pathology at the Wilhelmina Hospital in Vienna. His tenure at the hospital lasted twelve years, until March of 1920. During this time, he was at the height of his career and produced fifty-two papers on serological immunity, thirty-three on bacteriology and six on pathological anatomy.

He was among the first to dissociate antigens, which stimulate the production of immune responses known as antibodies, from the antibodies themselves. He was also among the first to purify antibodies, and his purification techniques are still used today for some applications in immunology.

Landsteiner also collaborated with Ernest Finger, the head of Vienna's Clinic for Venereal Diseases and Dermatology. In 1905, they successfully transferred the venereal disease syphilis from humans to apes. The result was that researchers had an animal model in which to study the disease.

In 1906, Landsteiner and Viktor Mucha, a scientist from the Chemical Institute at Finger's clinic, developed the technique of dark-field microscopy to identify and study the microorganisms that cause syphilis.

In 1930, Landsteiner received the Nobel Prize for Medicine for his work on differentiating the blood groups.

Landsteiner, along with A. S. Weiner, identified the Rh factor in 1940.

He died on June 26, 1943, of a heart attack while still working at his laboratory in New York.

◆◆◆

62

Antoine Laurent Lavoisier

(1743-1794)

Antoine-Laurent de Lavoisier, the father of modern chemistry, was a French noble prominent in the histories of chemistry and biology. He stated the first version of the law of conservation of mass, recognised and named oxygen (1778) and hydrogen (1783), abolished the phlogiston theory, helped construct the metric system, wrote the first extensive list of elements, and helped to reform chemical nomenclature.

Lavoisier was born in Paris on August 26, 1743.

He studied at the College Mazarin, in which he enrolled in 1754. At the College Mazarin he studied mathematics and astronomy with Nicolas de Lacaille, chemistry with Guillaume-Francois Rouelle and botany with Bernard de Jussieu. He received an outstanding education in language, literature, science and mathematics.

Following his family tradition, he pursued the study of law and he finished his education in the Faculty of Law in 1763.

He obtained his licence to practice law in 1764. But his inquiring mind took him to the world of science. First he studied geology under Jean Etienne Guettard, who was the first to prepare a geological map of France.

His methodical experiments and conviction that there was order in chemistry led him to develop the Law of Conservation of Mass. This stated that although chemicals may change state and appearance in a chemical reaction, there is no change in the quantity of matter. He showed this in his experiments in combustion. When he burnt phosphorous and sulphur he showed that the products weighed more than the original elements. He then undertook the same experiments in sealed containers and showed that the weight gained was lost from the air.

His experiments in combustion lead to much greater understanding of combustion and of the composition of air. At the time there was a popular theory of combustion called the 'phlogiston theory'. This suggested that all flammable substances contained a colourless, odourless, weightless substance called phlogiston which was given off when the substance was burned. He showed that in fact part of the air was responsible for combustion.

Lavoisier built on these discoveries when he discovered a 'flammable air' which produced water when burnt in air. He began modern chemistry nomenclature when he called this 'air' hydrogen, from the Greek for 'water-former'. He also named the part of air which supported combustion, 'oxygen'. These discoveries were committed to written form in 1789 when he wrote *Elementary Treatise of Chemistry*, considered to be the first modern chemistry textbook. He also proposed a definition of elements as a substance which could not be chemically broken down any further. He also suggested a list of elements including oxygen, nitrogen, hydrogen, phosphorous, mercury, zinc and sulphur. He did, however, include on his list of eiements both light and a substance called 'caloric' which was considered to be a weightless gas which was transferred from one body to another when heated.

Lavoisier was a remarkable man who contributed to the progress of chemistry in many ways, by his systematic methods and also by his remarkable insights into many areas of his field. He contributed to the development of a theory of chemical bonding and also showed that diamond was in fact a form of carbon. He also contributed to biology when he showed that the respiration of animals converted oxygen to carbon dioxide in the same way as burning.

Sadly, he was executed at the guillotine in May 1794 by French revolutionaries.

◆◆◆

63

Anton Van Leeuwenhoek

(1632-1723)

The Dutch naturalist and microscopist Anton van Leeuwenhoek, using simple microscopes of his own making, discovered bacteria, protozoa, spermatozoa, rotifers, Hydra and Volvox, and also parthenogenesis in aphids. He has rightly been called the father of microbiology.

Anton van Leeuwenhoek was born on October 24, 1632, at Delft, Holland.

His schooling was informal, probably including some mathematics and physical sciences but no languages. At the age of 16 he was sent to Amsterdam to become an apprentice at a linen draper's shop where he remained for about six years.

In 1654 van Leeuwenhoek returned to Delft and remained there for the rest of his life. In 1660 he was appointed chamberlain to the sheriffs of Delft, an office which he held for 39 years. Little is known of his activities for the next 13 years; however, in his spare time he must have begun to grind lenses to make simple microscopes.

Van Leeuwenhoek developed an interest in microscopes, which Zacharias Janssen had invented in 1590. As a hobby, he put together more than 247 simple ones—some of which were able to magnify objects 270 times. As early as 1668 he took one of his microscopes on a visit to England and used it to examine chalk from the cliffs in Kent.

Van Leeuwenhoek set out to study as many things as possible under his home-made microscopes. With his shaving razor he would slice off very thin slices of cork, plants or other specimens.

One summer he heard reports that nearby Lake Berkel had an unusually greenish, cloudy look to it. So he collected a water sample from the lake and placed it under one of his microscopes. He discovered a whole new world. There were little animals of various shapes and colors. He was the first scientist ever to give a detailed description of red blood cells (1675) and human spermatozoa (1677) or to see single-celled bacteria and protozoa. In 1683 he scraped some tartar off of his own teeth, looked at it under a microscope, and found living organisms.

All his observations were described in letters (at least 200), either to the Royal Society or to his friends. He never wrote a scientific paper or a book. His letters are full of random observations, with little coherence, and were written in a conversational style. Despite the casual way in which he described his observations, he never confused the facts with his speculations, and so it is possible to identify easily many of the organisms he studied from his detailed descriptions.

In 1673 Regnier de Graaf, a brilliant young physician of Delft, wrote a letter about Van Leeuwenhoek's work to Henry Oldenburg, Secretary of the Royal Society in London. This letter was published in *Philosophical Transactions*, and Oldenburg wrote to the author requesting further communications. Thus began a correspondence with the Royal Society which was to continue until van Leeuwenhoek's death.

The Royal Society elected him a fellow in 1680. His discoveries soon made him famous, and many came to visit him in Delft. His enthusiasm for the study of nature never waned even in old age, and despite his infirmities he still continued to make observations and send letters to the Royal Society.

After his death on Aug. 26, 1723, his daughter Maria sent a cabinet to the Royal Society which her father had prepared 22 years previously, containing 26 of his microscopes made from silver.

◆◆◆

64

Carl Linnaeus

(1707-1778)

Carl Linnaeus was a Swedish scientist who laid the foundations for the modern scheme of taxonomy. He is most widely known for having introduced efficient procedures for naming and classifying plants and animals at a time when new species were being rapidly discovered by explorers. He is also considered as one of the fathers of modern ecology.

Carl Linnaeus was born on May 23, 1707, at Rashult in Sweden.

The young Linnaeus showed a keen interest in plants and flowers and by the age of eight, was given the nickname 'the little botanist'. He began to study medicine at the University of Lund in 1727, transferring to the University of Uppsala the following year. He shared his passion for plants with Olaf Celsius whom he met at Uppsala.

Linnaeus headed an expedition to Lapland in 1732, travelling 4,600 miles and crossing the Scandinavian Peninsula by foot to the Arctic Ocean. On the journey he discovered a hundred botanical species.

In 1734, he mounted another expedition to central Sweden.

He undertook his medical degree in 1735 at the University of Harderwijk in Gelre, the Netherlands (which no longer exists), thence going to the University of Leiden for further studies.

After doctoring a short while for the navy, and having set up a Swedish Academy of Science, he arranged a seat at the

University of Uppsala, where he renovated the university's gardens and began teaching hugely popular courses in plant biology.

Also in 1735, he published *Systema Naturae*, his classification of plants based on their sexual parts. In his publications, he provided a concise, usable survey of all the world's plants and animals as then known, about 7,700 species of plants and 4,400 species of animals. These works helped to establish and standardise the consistent binomial nomenclature for species which he introduced on a world scale for plants in 1753, and for animals in 1758, and which is used today. His *Systema Naturae*, 10th edition, volume 1 (1758), has accordingly been accepted by international agreement as the official starting point for zoological nomenclature.

His method of binomial nomenclature using genus and species names was further expounded when he published *Fundamenta Botanica* (1736) and *Classes Plantarum* (1738). This system used the flower and the number and arrangements of its sexual organs of stamens and pistils to group plants into twenty-four classes which in turn are divided into orders, genera and species. He attempted to name and describe all known plants, calling each kind a species and assigning to each a two-part Greek or Latin name consisting of the genus (group) name followed by the species name. Many of his names of flowering plants survive with little, if any, change.

In 1738, he went to Stockholm to practise medicine and lecture, and became a professor at Uppsala University in 1741, attracting students from many countries to his often crowded lectures.

He was granted nobility in 1761, becoming Carl von Linné. He continued his work of classification and as a physician, and remained Rector of the University until 1772.

In that decade, he suffered from strokes, ill health, and memory loss until his death in 1778.

◆◆◆

65

Joseph Lister

(1827-1912)

Joseph Lister was a British surgeon, whose discovery of antiseptics in 1865 greatly reduced the number of deaths due to operating-room infections. He successfully introduced carbolic acid (phenol) to sterilise surgical instruments and to clean wounds.

Joseph Lister was born at Upton House, Upton, Essex, 5 April 1827, into a Quaker family.

He was educated at Grove House School, Tottenham, but because of his non-conformist religious beliefs, was excluded from Oxford and Cambridge universities as well as King's College, London, so he studied medicine at University College, London, which he entered in 1844.

Whilst still at school, he had decided to be a surgeon. He took the B.A. degree of the University of London in 1847, but, owing to an attack of smallpox, he did not begin his medical studies until the autumn of 1848.

On the completion of his career at University College, Lister went to Edinburgh in 1853, to work with the noted surgeon, James Syme. He decided to settle in Edinburgh, and in 1856, became assistant surgeon to the Royal Infirmary and took an active part in teaching in the extra-mural school, while continuing his researches on inflammation.

In 1860, he was appointed to the Chair of surgery in Glasgow University, and a year later became surgeon to the Glasgow Infirmary. It was here that he became deeply involved with antiseptics and made the observations and discoveries, which revolutionised the treatment of disease and injuries.

Influenced by the theories of Louis Pasteur, Lister began to experiment with chemical methods of preventing the infection of wounds by airborne bacilli. His early experiments involved the coating of wounds with a potent dose of carbolic, which formed an antiseptic crust of coagulated blood on the wound. The drawback of the carbolic acid treatment, however, was the toxicity of the acid. He was aware that the damage caused by the acid treatment could also damage the body's repair mechanisms. This led to the development of a number of antiseptic wound dressings designed to provide a disinfectant barrier between the wound and the surrounding air, while reducing to a minimum the carbolic acid entering the damaged tissue. He also introduced the sterilisation of surgical instruments with heat and carbolic acid and the frequent cleaning of the surgeon's hands during an operation with a mild antiseptic solution. He also introduced cleanliness for all operating rooms.

In 1867 Lister published two short but revolutionary papers, which introduced the principles of antiseptic surgery into medicine.

Another of Lister's major innovations was his introduction, in 1869, of cat-gut ligatures to replace the traditional silk thread, which was a major source of infection. His experiments showed that cat-gut ligatures were absorbed by the body and if soaked in carbolic acid could be made sterile.

In 1869, he became Professor of clinical surgery at Edinburgh and remained there until he was invited to King's College, London, in 1877. He filled the Chair of clinical surgery at King's College for fifteen years, and during the whole of this time was actively engaged in teaching and in pursuing his researches, besides practising as a surgeon and doing much public work.

Very soon his methods were applied to all kinds of surgical operations. The vanishing of septic diseases enlarged enormously the field of surgery, since operations formerly dreaded, owing to this risk, could now be carried out in safety.

The modern development of surgery was only possible as the result of his discoveries.

In 1883, Queen Victoria honoured Lister by making him Sir Joseph Lister. In 1897, he was given the title Lord Lister of Lyme Regis. He was first to be made a British peer for services to medicine. In 1902, he was given the Order of Merit, and made a Privy Councillor.

He took an active part in founding, in 1891, the British Institute of Preventive Medicine on the lines of the Pasteur Institute in Paris, and became its first chairman. In 1903, its name was changed to the Lister Institute of Preventive Medicine.

Joseph Lister died 10 February 1912. He was buried beside his wife, at the West Hampstead cemetery.

◆◆◆

66 Guglielmo Marchese Marconi

(1874-1937)

Marconi was a Nobel laureate physicist from Italy. He is best known for his invention of radio and he first introduced wireless telegraph system and radar.

Guglielmo Marconi was born in Bologna, Italy on April 25, 1874.

He did not go to school until he was twelve. His first school was in Florence. He was educated privately at Bologna, Florence and Leghorn. At the age of thirteen, he went to the Livorno Technical Institute where, for the first time, he heard formal lectures on physics and chemistry.

Soon, Marconi was spending most of his spare time studying and experimenting with electricity. Despite his father's disapproval, he continued to work on his experimental pursuits. To avoid confronting his father he chose a secret place in the garden to do his experiments.

Even as a boy he took a keen interest in physical and electrical science and studied the works of Maxwell, Hertz, Righi, Lodge and others.

In 1895 he began laboratory experiments at his father's country estate at Pontecchio where he succeeded in sending wireless signals over a distance of one and a half miles.

In 1896 he took his apparatus to England where he was introduced to Sir William Preece, Engineer-in-Chief of the Post

Office, and later that year was granted the world's first patent for a system of wireless telegraphy. He demonstrated his system successfully in London, on Salisbury Plain and across the Bristol Channel, and in July 1897 formed The Wireless Telegraph & Signal Company Limited (in 1900 re-named Marconi's Wireless Telegraph Company Limited).

In 1899 he established wireless communication between France and England across the English Channel. He erected permanent wireless stations at The Needles, Isle of Wight, at Bournemouth and later at the Haven Hotel, Poole, Dorset. Marconi went to United States of America to develop wireless communication across the world. He got its patent in his name. His wireless saved thousands of lives, on the ships of the sea in first decade of the twenty century.

In 1900 he took out his famous patent No. 7777 for 'tuned or syntonic telegraphy' and, on an historic day in December 1901, determined to prove that wireless waves were not affected by the curvature of the Earth, he used his system for transmitting the first wireless signals across the Atlantic between Poldhu, Cornwall, and St. John's, Newfoundland, a distance of 2,100 miles.

Between 1902 and 1912 he patented several new inventions. In 1902, during a voyage in the American liner *Philadelphia*, he first demonstrated 'daylight effect' relative to wireless communication and in the same year patented his magnetic detector which then became the standard wireless receiver for many years. By October 1926 shortwave stations began working in South Africa, India, Australia, United States and South America. His efforts helped in wireless communication in Aviation and Air force.

In December 1902 he transmitted the first complete messages to Poldhu from stations at Glace Bay, Nova Scotia, and later Cape Cod, Massachusetts, these early tests culminating in 1907 in the opening of the first transatlantic commercial service between Glace Bay and Clifden, Ireland, after the first shorter-distance public service of wireless telegraphy had been established between Bari in Italy and Avidari in Montenegro.

In 1905 he patented his horizontal directional aerial and in 1912 a 'timed spark' system for generating continuous waves.

In 1909 Marconi was awarded he Nobel Prize for physics jointly with Carl Braun of Germany.

In 1912 Marconi lost an eye. The same year he bought a ship *Elettra* and started a floating laboratory for a short wave research. Short wave, measuring ten-metre length needed smaller equipment. Ultra short waves measured in metres needed even smaller aerials. Throughout 1922 and 1923 he concentrated on shortwave wireless.

By October 1926 shortwave stations began working in South Africa, India, Australia, United States and South America.

In 1914 he was commissioned in the Italian Army as a Lieutenant being later promoted to Captain, and in 1916 transferred to the Navy in the rank of Commander. He was a member of the Italian Government mission to the United States in 1917 and in 1919 was appointed Italian plenipotentiary delegate to the Paris Peace Conference. He was awarded the Italian Military Medal in 1919 in recognition of his war service.

He has been the recipient of honorary doctorates of several universities and many other international honours and awards, among them the Nobel Prize for Physics, which in 1909 he shared with Professor Karl Braun, the Albert Medal of the Royal Society of Arts, the John Fritz Medal and the Kelvin Medal.

He was decorated by the Tsar of Russia with the Order of St. Anne, the King of Italy created him Commander of the Order of St. Maurice and St. Lazarus, and awarded him the Grand Cross of the Order of the Crown of Italy in 1902. Marconi also received the freedom of the City of Rome (1903), and was created Chevalier of the Civil Order of Savoy in 1905.

Many other distinctions of this kind followed. In 1914 he was both created a Senatore in the Italian Senate and appointed Honorary Knight Grand Cross of the Royal Victorian Order in England. He received the hereditary title of Marchese in 1929.

Marconi died in Rome on July 20, 1937.

67

James Clerk Maxwell

(1831-1879)

The Scottish physicist James, Clerk Maxwell, is credited with the most significant discovery of our age — the theory of electromagnetism. He is rightly acclaimed as the father of modern physics. He also made fundamental contributions to mathematics, astronomy and engineering.

James Clerk Maxwell was born in Edinburgh on 13 June 1831.

As a child, Maxwell was enrolled in the Edinburgh Academy.

Encouraged by his father and the natural philosopher James Forbes, the fourteen- year-old Maxwell produced his first publication: a paper describing a simple mechanical means of drawing mathematical curves with a piece of string. This combination of algebraic mathematics with elements of geometry would remain a distinctive feature of Maxwell's work.

At age 16, at the Edinburgh University, his studies there included Natural Philosophy, Moral Philosophy and Mental Philosophy.

Maxwell obtained his fellowship and graduated with a degree in mathematics from Trinity College in 1854.

In 1856, at the early age of 25, he became Professor of Physics at Marischal College, Aberdeen.

In 1860 he was appointed to the vacant chair of Natural Philosophy at King's College in London. The six years that he spent in this post were the years when he did his most important experimental work.

In London, around 1862, Maxwell calculated that the speed of propagation of an electromagnetic field is approximately that of the speed of light. He proposed that the phenomenon of light is therefore an electromagnetic phenomenon.

Maxwell also continued work he had begun at Aberdeen, considering the kinetic theory of gases. By treating gases statistically in 1866 he formulated, independently of Ludwig Boltzmann, the Maxwell-Boltzmann kinetic theory of gases. This theory showed that temperatures and heat involved only molecular movement.

From there he moved first to King's College, London, and then, in 1871, to become the first Professor of Experimental Physics at Cambridge where he directed the newly created Cavendish Laboratory. It was at the Cavendish, over the next fifty years, that so much of the physics of today continued to develop from Maxwell's inspiration.

Maxwell's first major contribution to science was a study of the planet Saturn's rings, the nature of which was much debated. He showed that stability could be achieved only if the rings consisted of numerous small solid particles, an explanation still accepted. He next considered molecules of gases in rapid motion. By treating them statistically he was able to formulate (1866), independently of Ludwig Boltzmann, the Maxwell-Boltzmann kinetic theory of gases. This theory showed that temperatures and heat involved only molecular movement.

In his research, conducted between 1864 and 1873, Maxwell showed that a few relatively simple mathematical equations could express the behaviour of electric and magnetic fields and their interrelated nature; that is, an oscillating electric charge produces an electromagnetic field. These four partial differential equations first appeared in fully developed form in *Electricity and Magnetism* (1873). Since known as Maxwell's equations they are one of the great achievements of 19th-century physics.

He died on November 5, 1879.

68

Gregor Johann Mendel

(1822-1884)

Mendel was an Austrian biologist, who, through his remarkable researches on hybridity in plants, established that there does exist, in living things, dominant and recessive characters (Mendelian Law).

Gregor Mendel was born in Heinzendorf, Austria on July 22, 1822.

His brilliant performance at school as a youngster encouraged his family to support his pursuit of a higher education, but their resources were limited.In 1843 he began studying at the St. Thomas Monastery of the Augustinian Order. In 1849, he was assigned to a secondary school in the city of Znaim.

In 1851 he entered the University of Vienna to train to be a teacher of Mathematics and Biology. It was at the University of Vienna that he developed his skills as a researcher which he utilised later in his life.

Mendel's attraction to research was based on his love of nature. He was not only interested in plants, but also in meteorology and theories of evolution. He often wondered how plants obtained atypical characteristics. On one of his frequent walks around the monastery, he found an atypical variety of an ornamental plant. He took it and planted it next to the typical variety. He grew their progeny side by side to see if there would be any approximation of the traits passed on to the next generation. He found that the plants' respective offspring retained the essential traits of the parents, and therefore were not influenced by the environment. This simple test gave birth to the idea of heredity.

During the middle of his life, Mendel did groundbreaking work into the theories of heredity. Using simple pea pod plants, he studied seven basic characteristics of the pea pod plants. By tracing these characteristics, he discovered three basic laws which governed the passage of a trait from one member of a species to another member of the same species. The first law states that the sex cells of a plant may contain two different traits, but not both of those traits. The second law stated that characteristics are inherited independently from another (the basis for recessive and dominant gene composition). The third theory states that each inherited characteristic is determined by two hereditary factors (known more recently as genes), one from each parents, which decides whether a gene is dominant or recessive. In other words, if a seed gene is recessive, it will not show up within the plant, however, the dominant trait will. Mendel's work and theories, later became the basis for the study of modern genetics, and are still recognised and used today.

From his studies, Mendel derived certain basic laws of heredity: hereditary factors do not combine, but are passed intact; each member of the parental generation transmits only half of its hereditary factors to each offspring; and different offspring of the same parents receive different sets of hereditary factors. His work became the foundation for modern genetics.

His work led to the discovery of particulate inheritance, dominant and recessive traits, genotype and phenotype, and the concept of heterozygous and homozygous.

Toward the end of his life, in 1868, Mendel was promoted in the monastery to Abbot.

He died on January 6, 1884.

◆◆◆

69

Dmitri Ivanovich Mendeleev (1834-1907)

Dmitri Mendeléev was Russian chemist who arranged the 63 known elements into a periodic table based on atomic mass, which he published in 'Principles of Chemistry' in 1869. His table placed elements in their correct position by atomic number, thus showing variance from atomic weight in a number of places.

Dmitri Ivanovich Mendeleev was born in the Siberian town of Tobol'sk in 1834.

He was not considered an outstanding student in his early education though he showed prowess in mathematics and science. After his father's death, he and his mother moved to St. Petersburg to pursue a university education. After being denied admission to both the University of Moscow and St. Petersburg University because of his provincial background and unexceptional academic background, he finally earned a place at the Main Pedagogical Institute (St. Petersburg Institute).

Upon graduation, Mendeleev took a position teaching science in a gymnasium. After a time as a teacher, he was admitted to graduate work at St. Petersburg University where he earned a Master's degree in 1856. He so impressed his instructors that he was retained to lecture in chemistry.

After spending 1859 and 1860 in Germany furthering his chemical studies, he secured a position as professor of chemistry at St. Petersburg University, a position he retained until 1890.

While writing a textbook on systematic inorganic chemistry, Principles of Chemistry, which appeared in thirteen editions the last being in 1947, Mendeleev organised his material in terms of the families of the known elements which displayed similar properties.

The first part of the text was devoted to the well known chemistry of the

Halogens. Next, he chose to cover the chemistry of the metallic elements in order of combining power — alkali metals first (combining power of one), alkaline earths (two), etc. However, it was difficult to classify metals such as copper and mercury which had multiple combining powers, sometimes one and other times two.

While trying to sort out this dilemma, Mendeleev noticed patterns in the properties and atomic weights of halogens, alkali metals and alkaline metals. In an effort to extend this pattern to other elements, he created a card for each of the 63 known elements. Each card contained the element's symbol, atomic weight and its characteristic chemical and physical properties.

When Mendeleev arranged the cards on a table in order of ascending atomic weight grouping elements of similar properties together in a manner not unlike the card arrangement in his favourite solitaire card game, patience, the periodic table was formed. From this table, he developed his statement of the periodic law and published his work *On the Relationship of the Properties of the Elements to their Atomic Weights* in 1869.

In 1906, Mendeleev came within one vote of being awarded the Nobel Prize for his work.

He died in 1907.

70

Hermann Minkowski

(1864-1909)

Hermann Minkowski was a was a German mathematician of Jewish and Polish descent, who developed the geometrical theory of numbers and who used geometrical methods to solve difficult problems in number theory, mathematical physics, and the theory of relativity.

Hermann Minkowski was born on June 22, 1864 in the town of Alexotas in what was once the Russian Empire (now Kaunas, Lithuania).

He was educated in Germany at the Universities of Berlin and Königsberg, where he achieved his doctorate in 1885. In 1883, when still 18, he was awarded the Grand Prix des Sciences Mathématiques of the Paris Academy of Sciences. The award was shared with Henry J. Smith for their work on the theory of quadratic forms.

Minkowski taught at the universities of Bonn, Göttingen, Königsberg and Zurich. In Zurich, he was one of Einstein's teachers

Minkowski explored the arithmetic of quadratic forms, especially concerning n variables, and his research into that topic led him to consider certain geometric properties in a space of n dimensions. In 1896, he presented his 'geometry of numbers', a geometrical method that solved problems in number theory.

In 1902, he joined the Mathematics Department of Göttingen in Germany, where he stayed for the rest of his life. It was in Göttingen that he entered into the field that would be his life's work. He learned mathematical physics from David Hilbert, and participated in a seminar on electron theory in 1905, and he learnt the latest results and theories in electrodynamics. .

By 1907 Minkowski realised that the special theory of relativity, introduced by Einstein in 1905 and based on previous work of Lorentz and Poincaré, could be best understood in a non-Euclidean space, since known as 'Minkowski space', in which the time and space are not separated entities but intermingled in a four dimensional space-time, and in which the Lorentz geometry of special relativity can be nicely represented. This 4-D treatment of electrodyinamics was published in his work *Raum und Zeit* (Time and Space) that same year, and provided the framework for later mathematical work in relativity. This nice representation certainly helped Einstein's quest for general relativity. The beginning part of his address delivered at the 80th Assembly of German Natural Scientists and Physicians (September 21, 1908) is now famous.

The asteroid 12493 Minkowski was named in his honour.

Hermann Minkowski died suddenly from a ruptured appendix in 1909, in Göttingen. He was 44.

◆◆◆

71

Thomas Hunt Morgan

(1866-1945)

The American zoologist and geneticist, Thomas Hunt Morgan, established the theory of the gene which helped clarify the process of evolution and formed the modern basis of heredity.

Thomas Hunt Morgan was born on September 25, 1866, in Lexington, Kentucky.

In 1886 he entered the State College of Kentucky and later studied at Johns Hopkins University, where he divided his time between morphology and physiology.

In 1890 he received his doctorate for a paper on the embryology and phylogeny of sea spiders.

In 1891 he served as professor of biology at Bryn Mawr College, after which he went to Europe for further study, first in Germany and then at the famous zoological station at Naples, Italy.

His early interests were in developmental biology and evolution. After moving to Columbia University in 1901 and coming under the influence of the great cell biologist Edwin Wilson, he turned his attention to understanding the physical basis of inheritance, which he saw as a means to test theories about the role of mutation in evolution.

In 1904, Morgan accepted a professorship at Columbia University which lasted until 1928. While there he undertook a series of breeding experiments to assess the reality of genes as the particles of heredity.

Morgan also gathered a trio of very bright students, Hermann Muller, Alfred Sturtevant, and Calvin Bridges, and cultivated an egalitarian system of collaboration that was unknown in most other labs.

Beginning in 1908, they proved that chromosomes do indeed carry the genes, that genes are discrete physical things arranged on chromosomes like beads on a string, that genes change places on chromosomes, that genes can be mutated and those mutations are faithfully inherited, and that mutations can be caused by exposure to high-energy radiation or other environmental phenomena.

Morgan chose the fruit fly (*Drosophila melanogaster*) for his experiments because it was a short-lived organism that could easily be bred in the laboratory under changing condition and could complete its life cycle in about 10 days, supplying as many as 30 generations a year.

Morgan's experiments were so successful that by 1914 he had proved the chromosome theory of heredity as a result of breeding and cytological examination.

In 1910 he found his first mutant and proceeded to cross this fly with a normal one. The percentages of normal and mutant offspring were in accordance with Mendel's law of inheritance. He found many mutant characters and soon discovered that certain characteristics not only were sex-linked but also tended to appear together in certain flies. From this he postulated that all sex-linked characters tended to be inherited together because they were associated as a unit on a single chromosome in the nucleus of the original cell. Morgan called these characters linkage groups.

By the summer of 1914 three linkage groups had been discovered. He used the word 'gene' to represent each character unit, and the exact positions of these genes in the chromosomes was worked out by Alfred Henry Sturtevant, one of his former students and a member of his research staff.

In 1915 Morgan and his assistants published *The Mechanism of Mendelian Heredity* to describe the system of genes. Later he published *The Theory of the Gene* (1926), his culminating work on the subject which discussed at length the chromosome theory of heredity.

In 1928 Morgan established the Kerckhoff Laboratories of Biological Sciences at the California Institute of Technology in Pasadena, which became the leading center for research genetics.

In 1933 he received the Nobel Prize in physiology or medicine in recognition of the significance of his theory of heredity for physiology and for the part that the new genetics was destined to play in the future of medicine. He shared the prize money with Sturtevant and Bridges.

Morgan was made a Foreign Member of the Royal Society of London in 1919, where he delivered the Croonian Lecture in 1922. In 1924, he was awarded the Darwin Medal, and in 1939 the Copley Medal of the Society.

In 1941 Morgan retired as active head of his department at Cal Tech. However, he continued to work on problems in embryology which he had first approached in 1903.

On December 4, 1945, the grand old man of genetics passed away.

◆◆◆

72

Samuel Finley Breese Morse

(1791-1872)

Samuel F. B. Morse developed lightning wires and Morse code, an electronic alphabet that could carry messages. A line was constructed between Baltimore and Washington and the first message, sent on May 24, 1844, was 'What hath God wrought!' In 1861 the two coasts of the United States were linked by telegraph.

Samuel Finley Breese Morse was born in Charlestown, Massachusetts on April 27, 1791.

Since the age of four, Morse had been interested in drawing. When he was fourteen, he earned pocket money by drawing pictures of his friends and people in the town.

As a student at Yale College, Morse became interested in both painting and in the developing subject of electricity. After his graduation in 1810, he first concentrated on painting, which he studied in England.

After moving to New York in 1825, he became a founder and the first president of the National Academy of Design. He maintained a steady interest in invention, taking out three patents for pumps in 1817 with his brother Sidney Edwards Morse. It wasn't until 1832 that he first became interested in telegraphy.

That year, Morse was travelling to the United States from Europe on a ship, when he overheard a conversation about electromagnetism that inspired his idea for an electric telegraph.

Though he had little training in electricity, he realised that pulses of electrical current could convey information over wires. Around that time two German engineers had invented a five-wire model, but Morse wanted to be the first to reduce the number of wires to one.

Between 1832 and 1837 he developed a working model of an electric telegraph, using crude materials such as a home-made battery and old clock-work gears. He also acquired two partners to help him develop his telegraph: Leonard Gale, a professor of science at New York University, and Alfred Vail, who made available his mechanical skills and his family's New Jersey iron works to help construct better telegraph models.

Morse's first telegraph device, unveiled in 1837, did use a one-wire system, which produced an EKG-like line on tickertape. By the following year he had developed an improved system, having created a dot-and-dash code that used different numbers to represent the letters of the English alphabet and the ten digits. This coding system was significantly better, as it did not require printing or decoding, but could be 'sound read' by operators. In 1838, at an exhibition of his telegraph in New York, Morse transmitted ten words per minute using the Morse code that would become standard throughout the world.

In 1849, Morse was granted a patent of the printing telegraph. On May 11, 1844, he sent the first inter-city message. Soon thereafter, he gave the first public demonstration, in which he sent a message from the chamber of the Supreme Court to the Mount Clair train depot in Baltimore.

By 1846, private companies, using Morse's patent, had built telegraph lines from Washington to Boston and Buffalo, and were pushing further. The telegraph spread across the US more quickly than had the railroads, whose routes the wires often followed. By 1854, there were 23,000 miles of telegraph wire in operation. Western Union was founded in 1851, and in 1866, the first successful trans-Atlantic cable link was established.

Morse died of pneumonia in New York on April 2, 1872.

◆◆◆

73

John Von Neumann

(1903-1957)

John von Neumann, a great Hungarian mathematician and physicist, was an early pioneer in fields such as game theory, nuclear deterrence, and modern computing.

Jon von Neumann was born on December 28, 1903, in Budapest, the capital of Hungary.

At a very young age, Neumann was interested in math, the nature of numbers and the logic of the world around him. At age eight he became fascinated by history and read all forty-four volumes of the universal history, which resided in the family's library. Even this early, heshowed that he was comfortable applying his mind to both the logical and social world.

In 1914, at the age of 10, Neumann's educational road to the university started at the Lutheran Gymnasium. His first paper was published in 1922, when he was 17, in the *Journal of the German Mathematical Society,* dealing with the zeros of certain minimal polynomials.

In 1921 Neumann was sent to become a chemical engineer at the University of Berlin and then to Zurich two years later. During this time of practical undergraduate study, he was executing another plan that was more in tune with his interests. In the summer after his studies at Berlin and before he went to Zurich he enrolled at the Budapest University as a candidate for an advanced doctorate in mathematics.

Von Neumann breezed through his two years at Berlin and then set himself to the work on chemical engineering at the ETH and his mathematical studies in Budapest. He worked on his set theory thesis in Zurich while completing classes for the ETH. After finishing his thesis he took the final exams in Budapest to receive his Ph.D. with highest honours. This was just after his graduation from the ETH, so in 1926 he had two degrees, one an undergraduate degree in chemical engineering and the other a Ph.D. in mathematics, all by the time he was twenty-two.

Von Neumann's two main contributions to the Los Alamos project were the mathematicisation of development and his contributions to the implosion bomb. The scientists at Los Alamos were used to doing scientific experiments but it is difficult to do many experiments when developing weapons of mass destruction. They needed some way to predict what was going to happen in these complex reactions without actually performing them. He therefore was a member of the team that invented modern mathematical modelling. Although he did not arrive first at the implosion technique for plutonium, he was the one who made it work, developing the 'implosion lens' of high explosives that would correctly compress the plutonium.

Von Neumann's experience with mathematical modelling at Los Alamos, and the computational tools he used there, gave him the experience he needed to push the development of the computer. With his contributions to the architecture of the computer, which describe how logical operations are represented by numbers that can then be read and processed, many of his dreams have come true. Today we have extremely powerful computing machines used in scores of scientific fields, as well many more non-scientific fields.

His primary area of interest, however, centered on game theory: the study of the conflict between two opponents seeking to arrive at two different goals, each wishing to beat the other.

He is also credited with at least one contribution to the study of algorithms. Donald Knuth cites von Neumann as the inventor, in 1945, of the well-known merge sort algorithm, in which the first and second halves of an array are each sorted recursively and then merged together. He also engaged in exploration of problems in the field of numerical hydrodynamics.

As director of the Electronic Computer Project at Princeton's Institute for Advanced Study (1945-1955), he developed MANIAC (mathematical analyser, numerical integrator and computer), which at the time was the fastest computer of its kind. Built at a time long before the invention of the silicon chip, MANIAC was run on thousands of vacuum tubes.

In 1955 he was named a Commissioner of the Atomic Energy Commission, a position he held up to his death, and in 1956 he received its Enrico Fermi Award.

He died from cancer on February 8, 1957, in Washington, D.C.

74

Sir Isaac Newton

(1642-1727)

Isaac Newton was the greatest English mathematician of his generation. He laid the foundation for differential and integral calculus. His work on optics and gravitation make him one of the greatest scientists the world has known

Isaac Newton was born in the manor house of Woolsthorpe, near Grantham in Lincolnshire on December 25, 1642.

In 1653, Newton began attending the Free Grammar School in Grantham. His school reports described him as 'idle' and 'inattentive'. He was taken away from school but was allowed to return to it in Grantham in 1660 to complete his school education.

Newton entered his uncle's old College, Trinity College Cambridge, on 5 June 1661. His interest in mathematics began in the autumn of 1663 when he bought an astrology book at a fair in Cambridge and Barrow's edition of *Euclid's Elements.*

Newton received his bachelor's degree in April 1665. When the plague closed the University in the summer of 1665 he had to return to Lincolnshire. There, in a period of less than two years, while he was still under 25 years old, he began revolutionary advances in mathematics, optics, physics and astronomy.

When the University of Cambridge reopened after the plague in 1667, Newton was elected to a minor fellowship at Trinity College but, after being awarded his Master's Degree, he was elected to a major fellowship in July 1668 which allowed him to dine at the Fellows' Table. In July 1669 Barrow sent Newton's text *De Analysi* to Collins in London.

In 1672 Newton was elected a fellow of the Royal Society after donating a reflecting telescope. Also in 1672 he published his first scientific paper on light and colour in the *Philosophical Transactions of the Royal Society*. His *Opticks* appeared in 1704. It dealt with the theory of light and colour and with investigations of the colours of thin sheets 'Newton's rings' and diffraction of light.

In 1687 he published the *Philosophiae naturalis principia mathematica* or *Principia* as it is always known. The *Principia* is recognised as the greatest scientific book ever written. Newton analysed the motion of bodies in resisting and non-resisting media under the action of centripetal forces. The results were applied to orbiting bodies, projectiles, pendulums and free-fall near the Earth. He further demonstrated that the planets were attracted toward the Sun by a force varying as the inverse square of the distance and generalised that all heavenly bodies mutually attract one another.

Newton explained a wide range of previously unrelated phenomena: the eccentric orbits of comets, the tides and their variations, the precession of the Earth's axis, and motion of the Moon as perturbed by the gravity of the Sun. This work made him an international leader in scientific research.

After suffering a second nervous breakdown in 1693, Newton retired from research. He decided to leave Cambridge to take up a government position in London becoming Warden of the Royal Mint in 1696 and Master in 1699. However, he did not resign his positions at Cambridge until 1701.

In 1703 he was elected president of the Royal Society and was re-elected each year until his death. He was knighted in 1705 by Queen Anne, the first scientist to be so honoured for his work.

Sadly, he died in 1727 in Westminster Abbey.

◆◆◆

75

Marshall W. Nirenberg

(1927-)

Nirenberg's research helped to unravel the DNA genetic code, aiding in the determination of which genes code for certain hereditary traits. For his contribution to the sciences of genetics and cell biochemistry, Nirenberg was awarded the 1968 Nobel Prize in physiology or medicine with Robert W. Holley and Har Gobind Khorana.

Nirenberg was born in New York City on April 10, 1927.

In 1944 he enrolled at the University of Florida, studying zoology and botany, subjects that had long interested him. Whilst still an undergraduate he worked as a laboratory assistant and even as a teaching assistant; and while working in the Nutrition Laboratory he was introduced to biochemistry, then little studied at the undergraduate level. He learned how to use radioactive isotopes to follow the course of biochemical reactions, a technique that was to prove vital to his later research.

He earned his B.S. in 1948 and his M.Sc. in biology in 1952 from the University of Florida. His interest in science extended beyond his formal studies. For two of his undergraduate years he worked as a teaching assistant in biology, and he also spent a brief period as a research assistant in the nutrition laboratory.

In 1952, Nirenberg continued his graduate studies at the University of Michigan, this time in the field of biochemistry.

Obtaining his Ph.D. in 1957, he wrote his dissertation on the uptake of hexose, a sugar molecule, by ascites tumour cells.

Shortly after earning his Ph.D., Nirenberg began his investigation into the inner workings of the genetic code as an American Cancer Society (ACS) fellow at the National Institutes of Health (NIH) in Bethesda, Maryland. He continued his research at the NIH after the ACS fellowship ended in 1959, under another fellowship from the Public Health Service (PHS). In 1960, when the PHS fellowship ended, he joined the NIH staff permanently as a research scientist in biochemistry.

After only a brief time conducting research at the NIH, Nirenberg made his mark in genetic research with the most important scientific breakthrough since James D. Watson and Francis Crick discovered the structure of DNA in 1953. Specifically, he discovered the process for unraveling the code of DNA. This process allows scientists to determine the genetic basis of particular hereditary traits.

In August of 1961, Nirenberg announced his discovery during a routine presentation of a research paper at a meeting of the International Congress of Biochemistry in Moscow.

Nirenberg's research involved the genetic code sequences for amino acids. He discovered how to determine which sequences patterns code for which amino acids (there are about 20 known amino acids).

Nirenberg's discovery has led to a better understanding of genetically determined diseases and, more controversially, to further research into the controlling of hereditary traits; or genetic engineering. For his research, he was awarded the 1968 Nobel Prize for physiology or medicine. He shared the honour with scientists Har Gobind Khorana and Robert W. Holley.

After receiving the Nobel Prize, Nirenberg switched his research focus to other areas of biochemistry, including cellular control mechanisms and the cell differentiation process.

Since first being hired by the NIH in 1960, Nirenberg has served in different capacities. From 1962 until 1966 he was Head of the Section for Biochemical Genetics, National Heart Institute. Since 1966 he has been serving as the Chief of the Laboratory of Biochemical Genetics, National Heart, Lung and Blood Institute.

Other honours bestowed upon Nirenberg, in addition to the Nobel Prize, include honorary membership in the Harvey Society, the Molecular Biology Award from the National Academy of Sciences (1962), National Medal of Science presented by President Lyndon B. Johnson (1965), and the Louisa Gross Horwitz Prize for Biochemistry (1968). Nirenberg also received numerous honorary degrees from distinguished universities, including the University of Michigan (1965), University of Chicago (1965), Yale University (1965), University of Windsor (1966), George Washington University (1972), and the Weizmann Institute in Israel (1978).

Nirenberg is a member of several professional societies, including the National Academy of Sciences, the Pontifical Academy of Sciences, the American Chemical Society, the Biophysical Society, and the Society for Developmental Biology.

He has continued to work on the very complex problems of understanding how genetic information controls the development and metabolism of living organisms.

◆◆◆

76

Blaise Pascal

(1623-1662)

Blaise Pascal was a French mathematician, physicist, and theologian. His early work included the invention of the adding machine and syringe, and the co-development with Fermat of the mathematical theory of probability. He was the inventor of the first digital calculator.

Blaise Pascal was born in 1623 in Clermont-Ferrand, Auvergne (now Clermont-Ferrand) France.

He studied privately, tutored mostly by his father, Etienne, who was a scientist and a government official. From an early age Pascal showed an inclination toward mathematics. He wrote at the age of 16 a highly appreciated treatise, *Essay Pour les Conigues.*

Together with Pierre de Fermat, Pascal invented the calculus of probabilities and laid the foundations for Gottfried Wilhelm von Leibniz's infinitesimal calculus.

In 1647 Pascal invented a calculating machine, becoming one of the fathers of the Computer Age — and later the barometer, the hydraulic press, and the syringe. While still a teenager, he invented the first machine to do calculations—an arithmetic machine which could add and subtract. Although expensive to make and difficult to operate, Pascal's calculating machine was an essential step in the subsequent development of calculators and computers.

Pascal continued his work in science and mathematics. His experiments with the barometer proved the now familiar facts that atmospheric pressure decreases as altitude increases, and also changes as the weather changes. He made a valuable contribution to developing both hydrostatics and hydrodynamics. He showed that the pressure applied to a confined liquid is transmitted undiminished through the liquid in all directions, regardless of the area to which the pressure is applied. This is known as Pascal's Law and is the principle behind the hydraulic press, which Pascal designed. During these experiments with fluids, he invented the syringe.

Pascal also investigated the cycloid—the curve formed by a point on the circumference of a circle as the circle rolls along a straight line. His discovery of many physical and mathematical properties of the cycloid was an important step towards the later development of calculus by others.

Pascal also worked with another mathematician, Fermat, on the Theory of Probability. Although their investigations were carried out on various gambling situations, this theory has an immense number of applications. It is the basis of all insurance schemes and it is of great value to many other branches of science such as quantum physics, where the behaviour of particles can be described using probabilities. He invented a simple method now known as Pascal's Triangle to determine the probability of certain outcomes.

Pascal's other important scientific contributions include his investigations in the geometry of infinitesimal. His methodology reflected his emphasis on empirical experimentation as opposed to analytical, a priori methods, and he believed that human progress is perpetuated by the accumulation of scientific discoveries resulting from such experimentation.

In Clermont Pascal demonstrated how the weight of the Earth's atmosphere balanced the mercury in the barometer.

Until 1654 he devoted himself to mathematics and scientific studies.

Pascal died on 19 August 1662, in Paris.

◆◆◆

77

Louis Pasteur

(1822-1895)

Louis Pasteur, a Frech chemist and bacteriologist, was a pioneer in the fields of bacteriology and preventive medicine. He is the founder of microbiology.

Louis Pasteur was born on December 27, 1822, in the small town of Dole, France.

He studied in the college of Arbois and at Besancon, where he graduated in arts in 1840.

For his doctorate his attention was directed to the then obscure science of crystallography. This was to have a decisive influence on his carrer.

Pasteur, under special dispensation from the minister of education, recieved a leave of absence from his duties as professor of physics at the lycee of Tournon to pursue research on the optical properties of crystals of the salts of tartrates and paratartrates, which had the capacity to rotate the plane of polarised light.

This early research of the chemical studies of the tartrates led him to the discovery (1848) of molecular dissymmetry.

He prepared 19 different salts, examined these under a microscope, and determined that they possessed hemihedral facets. However, the crystal faces were oriented differently; they were left-handed or right-handed, thus having the asymmetrical relationship of mirror images. Furthermore, each geometric variety of crystal rotated the light in accordance with its structure, while equal mixtures of the left-and right-handed crystals had no optical activity in as much as the physical effects canceled each other. Thus he demonstrated the phenomenon of optical isomers. The french government made him a member of the Legion of Honor, and Britain's Royal Society presented him with the 'Copley Medal'.

He had already established an international reputation as a chemist and won the 'Rumford Medal' of the British Royal.

He then began work on fermentation, which had important results. His experiments with bacteria conclusively disproved (1862) the theory of spontaneous generation and let to the germ theory of infection.

His work on wine, vinegar and beer resulted in the development of the process of pasteurisation.

Of great economic value also was his solution for the control of silkworm disease, his study of chicken cholera, and his technique of vaccination against anthrax, which was succesfully administered against rabies in 1885.

In 1888 the Pasteur Institute was founded in Paris, with Pasteur as its director, to continue work on rabies and to provide a teaching and research centre on virulent and contagious diseases.

On September 28, 1895, honoured by the world but unspoiled and overflowing with affection, Pasteur died near Saint-Cloud.

◆◆◆

78

Max Karl Ernst Ludwig Planck

(1867-1934)

The German physicist, Max Karl Ernst Ludwig Planck developed the concept of the quantum, or fundamental increment of energy, basic to quantum mechanics, and a cornerstone of modern physics.

Max Planck, the son of a professor of law, was born in Kiel, Germany, on 23rd April, 1858.

Max Planck began his elementary schooling in Kiel. As a young student he had shown great promise in music, but a remarkable mathematics teacher turned his interest toward science. In the spring of 1867 his family moved to Munich when his father was appointed Professor there. He attended secondary school there, entering the famous Maximilian Gymnasium in May 1867.

In July 1874, at the age of 16, he passed his school leaving examination with distinction

He studied physics at the University of Munich (1874-1877) and the University of Berlin (1877-78) before receiving his doctorate in 1879 at the age of 21. After gaining degrees from the Universities of Berlin and Munich, he focused on thermodynamics. He was especially interested in the nature of radiation from hot materials.

On 2 May 1885 Planck was appointed extraordinary professor of theoretical physics in Kiel and held this chair for four years. He now worked on thermodynamics publishing three excellent papers on applications to physical chemistry and thermoelectricity.

Planck was appointed as an extraordinary professor of theoretical physics at the University of Berlin on 29 November 1888, at the same time became director of the Institute for Theoretical Physics. He was promoted to ordinary professor on 23 May 1892 and held the chair until he retired on 1 October 1927.

While in Berlin Planck did his most brilliant work and delivered outstanding lectures. He studied thermodynamics, in particular examining the distribution of energy according to wavelength. By combining the formulae of Wien and Rayleigh, he announced in October 1900 a formula now known as Planck's radiation formula. Within two months he made a complete theoretical deduction of his formula renouncing classical physics and introducing the quanta of energy.

In 1901 he devised a theory that perfectly described the experimental evidence, but part of it was a radical new idea: energy did not flow in a steady continuum, but was delivered in discrete packets Planck later called quanta, the magnitudes of which are proportional to the frequency of the radiation. Though it sounded outlandish, applying this idea to the problem of heated bodies revealed a simple relationship that explained previous puzzles. He found that the energy radiated from a heated body is exactly proportional to the wavelength of its radiation. So, a black body would not radiate all frequencies equally. As temperature goes up, energy increases and it's more likely that quanta with higher energy will be radiated. So, as an object heats up, the light given off is orange, then yellow, and eventually bluish. The wavelength emitted is a function of the energy times a constant (h), now known as Planck's constant. That explained why, for example, a hot iron poker glows distinctly red and white.

Though Planck's idea was not immediately believed by most physicists, it is now accepted as one of the fundamental constants in the universe. In fact, he himself wasn't sure if it was more than a little mathematics that resolved his own particular problem. Scientists such as Albert Einstein, Niels Bohr, and

Werner Heisenberg shaped modern physics by applying his elegantly simple, catalytic new idea. Albert Einstein used Planck's quantum theory to explain photoelectricity and Niels Bohr successfully applied the quantum theory to the atom.

He taught at the University of Munich before being appointed associate professor at the University of Kiel.

In 1918 Planck was awarded the Nobel Prize for Physics.

Planck was much involved with the German Physical Society, being treasurer and a committee member. He was chairman of the Society from 1905 to 1908 and then again from 1915 to 1916. He was also honoured by being elected an honorary member in 1927. Two years later an award, the Max Planck Medal, was established and Planck himself became the first recipient.

In 1930 he was appointed as president of the Kaiser Wilhelm Institute in 1930. An opponent of Adolf Hitler, Planck resigned his position in 1937 in protest against the decision by Bernard Rust, the minister of education, to sack Jewish teachers from Germany's universities. After the war, the research centre was renamed the Max Planck Institute and he was appointed its head.

Max Planck died on 4 October, 1947.

◆◆◆

79

Joseph Priestley

(1733-1804)

Joseph Priestley was an 18th-century British theologian, dissenting clergyman, natural philosopher, educator and political theorist who published over 150 works. He is usually credited with the discovery of oxygen, having isolated it in its gaseous state, although Carl Wilhelm Scheele and Antoine Lavoisier also have a claim to the discovery.

Joseph Priestley was born at Fieldhead in Birstall Parish, Leeds in 1733.

At the grammar school he entered in 1745, Priestley learned Latin, Greek and improved on a system of shorthand, but after three years ill-health forced him to return home. He was a brilliant student and with the help of local teachers, he became proficient in physics, philosophy, algebra, mathematics and several different languages.

After his health improved, Priestley entered the new nonconformist Daventry Academy in Northamptonshire, where he studied history, science and philosophy. At Daventry he read David Hartley's *Observations of Man* (1749). He was deeply influenced by Hartley's views on free will and the notion of human perfectibility through good education.

In 1755 he became minister at a small Presbyterian parish at Needham Market, Suffolk, and there wrote *The Scripture Doctrine of Remission.*

Three years later he moved to Nantwich in Cheshire. He opened a small school where he developed his ideas on education. He was especially interested in exploring how science could improve the quality of human life.

In 1761 Priestley was appointed as tutor at the dissenting Warrington Academy in Lancashire. His *Chart of Biography* (1765) won him a doctorate of laws from the University of Edinburgh and his experiments in electricity brought him into the Royal Society in 1766.

While at Warrington Priestley wrote *Liberal Education for Civil and Active Life* (1765). In the book he stressed the importance of science, arts, modern languages and history and argued they were better suited than the classics for those students who wanted a career in industry and commerce. This was followed by *The History and Present State of Electricity* (1767).

In preparing the publication Priestley began to perform experiments—at first merely to reproduce those reported in the literature but later to answer questions of his own. In the 1770s he began his most famous scientific research on the nature and properties of gases. At that time he was living next to a brewery, which provided him an ample supply of carbon dioxide. His first chemical publication was a description of how to carbonate water, in imitation of some naturally occurring bubbly mineral waters. He began examining all the 'airs' that might be released from different substances. By clever design of apparatus and careful manipulation, he isolated and characterised eight gases, including oxygen—a record not equalled before or since.

In 1772 he published *The History of the Present State of the Discoveries relating to Vision, Light and Colours* as the first volume of a projected multi-volume series on the history of experimental philosophy.

In 1772, he presented the paper, *On Different Kinds of Air*, to the Royal Society. It was this paper which established his reputation as a chemist. Two years later he prepared the first edition of *Experiments and Observations on Different Kinds of Air*, which he republished a number of times until 1790.

Priestley differentiated between nine gases — only three of which were previously known to science. Of particular significance was 'dephlogisticated air' (oxygen) which he produced on August 1, 1774, by heating red mercuric oxide. It then became clear that air was not an element. He isolated oxygen and observed its importance in combustion, but it was left to Cavendish and Lavoisier to appreciate the theoretical significance of his work.

In addition, he contributed to the understanding of photosynthesis and respiration.

Priestley now turned his attention to politics. In 1768 his book *The First Principles of Government and the Nature of Political, Civil and Religious Liberty* was published. In it he argued for the development of a political system that maximises civil liberty.

Priestley moved to Birmingham where he became friends with businessmen and scientists. Whereas his scientific work, for example, his discovery of oxygen, was welcomed, his religious and political views were constantly getting him into trouble.

His predictions that the French Revolution heralded a change in the role of the monarchy upset King George III. The king and his supporters particularly disliked his view that in future monarchs will be the "first servants of the people and accountable to them". Priestley now obtained the nickname 'Gunpowder'.

After the Birmingham riots Priestley moved to London where he taught history and science at New College, Hackney.

He was elected to the French Academy of Sciences in 1772 and to the St. Petersburg Academy in 1780. He became in that year minister of a chapel in Birmingham.

In 1774 he decided to emigrate to America. He settled in Pennsylvania and over the next few years he wrote several books on Unitarianism. He also established the first Unitarian Church in America.

Joseph Priestley died in Northumberland on 6 February, 1804, and was buried there in a Quaker burial ground.

◆◆◆

80 Sir Chandrashekhara Venkata Raman

(1888-1970)

Bharat Ratna and Nobel Prize winner, Sir Chandrasekhara Venkata Raman, is known for his work on the scattering of light and for the discovery of the Raman effect, named after him. He received the 1930 Nobel Prize in Physics for his work.

Chandrashekhara Venkata Raman was born on November 7, 1888 in Tiruchirapalli, Tamil Nadu.

He completed his Bachelors and Masters degrees from Presidency College, Madras, winning the first place and the gold medal in physics. In 1907, he passed his M.A. obtaining the highest distinctions

Shortly thereafter, he joined the Indian Finance Department as an Assistant Accountant General in Calcutta. After his office hours, he carried out his experimental research in the laboratory of the Indian Association for the Cultivation of Science at Calcutta. He carried out research in acoustics of musical instruments and optics.

Later, he started doing experiments at the Indian Association for the Cultivation of Science (IACS).

In 1917, Raman resigned from his government service and took up the newly created post of Sir Taraknath Palit Professorship in Physics at the University of Calcutta. At the same time, he continued with his research at IACS. He stayed there for the next fifteen years. During his tenure there, he received worldwide recognition for his work in optics and scattering of light.

He was elected to the Royal Society of London in 1924 and the British made him a knight of the British Empire in 1929.

He presided over the 16th session of the Indian Science Congress in 1929.

He was elected a Fellow of the Royal Society early in his career (1924), and was knighted in 1929.

In 1930, Raman was awarded the Nobel Prize in Physics for his work on scattering of light. The discovery was later named 'Raman Effect'.

In 1934, Raman became the director of the newly established Indian Institute of Sciences in Bangalore, where two years later he continued as a professor of physics. Other investigations carried out by him were: his experimental and theoretical studies on the diffraction of light by acoustic waves of ultrasonic and hypersonic frequencies (published 1934-1942), and those on the effects produced by X-rays on infrared vibrations in crystals exposed to ordinary light.

In 1947, he was appointed as the first National Professor by the new government of Independent India. He retired from the Indian Institute in 1948 and a year later he established the Raman Research Institute in Bangalore, where he worked till his death.

He was awarded the Bharat Ratna in 1954 and received the Lenin Peace Prize in 1957.

The government has honoured Sir CV Raman by declaring 28th February every year as National Science Day to commemorate Raman's discovery in 1928.

Sir C.V. Raman died on November 21, 1970.

◆◆◆

81 Srinivasa Ramanujan Iyengar

(1887-1920)

The Indian mathematician, Srinivasa Ramanujan Iyengar, is best known for his work on hypergeometric series and continued fractions. He made substantial contributions in the areas of mathematical analysis, number theory, infinite series and continued fractions.

Srinivasa Ramanujan was born at Erode on December 22, 1887.

At age ten he demonstrated a natural ability at maths, and was given books on advanced trigonometry by S.L. Loney. By the time he was 13, he could solve unaided every problem in *Loney's Trigonometry*, and at 14 he obtained the theorems for the sine and the cosine that had been anticipated by L. Euler. He mastered this book, and even discovered theorems of his own. He showed unusual mathematical skills at school, winning accolades and awards.

In 1903 he came upon George Shoobridge Carr's *Synopsis of Elementary Results in Pure and Applied Mathematics*. The book, opened a whole new world to him, and he set out to establish the 6,165 theorems in it for himself. Having no contact with good books, he had to do original research for each solution. Trying to devise his own methods, he made some astounding discoveries, among them several new algebraic series.

By the age of seventeen, Ramanujan was conducting his own mathematical research on Bernoulli numbers and the Euler–

Mascheroni constant. He received a scholarship to study at Government College in Kumbakonam.

To make a living, he worked as a clerk in the accountant general's office at the Madras Port Trust Office.

In 1912-1913, Ramanujan sent samples of his theorems to three academics at University of Cambridge. Only G. H. Hardy a prominent English mathematician recognised his brilliant work, and he asked to him study under him at Cambridge.

In 1914 Ramanujan went to Cambridge. The university experience gave him considerable sophistication, but his mind, by this time somewhat hardened, generally continued to work according to the old pattern, in which intuition played a more important role than argument. In Hardy's opinion, if Ramanujan's gift had been recognised early, he could have become one of the greatest mathematicians of all time. In hypergeometric series and continued fractions, he was unquestionably one of the great masters. His patience, memory, power of calculation, and intuition made him the greatest formalist of his day.

Ramanujan independently compiled nearly 3,900 results (mostly identities and equations) during his short lifetime. Most of his claims have now been proven to be correct. He stated results that were both original and highly unconventional, such as the Ramanujan prime and the Ramanujan theta function, and these have inspired a vast amount of further research. Recently, his formulae have found applications in the field of crystallography and in string theory.

The *Ramanujan Journal*, an international publication, was launched to publish work in all the areas of mathematics that were influenced by Ramanujan.

In 1918 Ramanujan was elected a fellow of the Royal Society and a Fellow of Trinity College, Cambridge.

He died on April 26, 1920.

◆◆◆

82

Charles Francis Richter
(1900-1985)

With German-born seismologist Beno Gutenberg, Charles Richter developed the scale that bears his name and measures the magnitude of earthquakes. He was a pioneer in seismological research at a time when data on the size and location of earthquakes were scarce. He authored two textbooks that are still used as references in the field and are regarded by many scientists as his greatest contribution, exceeding the more popular Richter scale.

Charles Francis Richter was born on a farm near Hamilton, Ohio, north of Cincinnati, on April 26, 1900.

He attended a preparatory school associated with the University of Southern California, which he attended for his freshman year. He obtained his from Standford University, Bachelor's degree in physics in 1920 and his Ph.D. in theoretical physics from the California Institute of Technology in 1928.

Richter got a job as a research assistant at the newly established Seismological Laboratory in Pasadena, then managed by the Carnegie Institution of Washington. Thus he started applying his physics background to the study of the earth.

Here he teamed with laboratory director Beno Gutenberg to develop a method for measuring earthquake intensity that accurately reflected earthquake strength. The Richter Scale, which was published in 1935, used a seismograph to record actual earth motion during an earthquake. The scale takes into account the instrument's distance from the epicenter, or the point on the ground that is directly above the earthquake's origin. Richter chose to use the term 'magnitude' to describe an earthquake's strength because of his early interest in astronomy; stargazers use the word to describe the brightness of stars. The Richter Scale became the standard almost immediately, and remains so to this day.

Richter and Gutenberg continued to work together for several decades, monitoring and measuring seismic activity around the world. In the late 1930's, the two applied their scale to deep earthquakes (those occurring more than 185 miles below ground). In 1941, they published *Seismicity of the Earth*, which remained a standard seismology textbook for decades. They also worked on locating the epicenters of all major earthquakes, and on classifying them into geographical groups.

Richter also did much to improve the chances of human survival in a major earthquake. He was intimately involved in promoting improved building codes in earthquake-prone areas, and was often quick to emphasize that much loss of life in earthquakes is due to building collapses.

In 1952, Richter became a full professor of seismology at Cal Tech, where he remained the rest of his career, except for a visit to the University of Tokyo from 1959 to 1960 as a Fulbright scholar. His most important work, *Elementary Seismology*, was published in 1958. The book contained detailed descriptions of major historical earthquakes, tables and charts, and discussions on earthquake motion, earthquake insurance, and building construction in earthquake-prone areas.

After retiring from Cal Tech in 1970, he helped start a seismic consulting firm that evaluated buildings for the government, public utilities, and private businesses. He was also instrumental in establishing the Southern California Seismic Array, a network of instruments that has helped scientists track the origin and intensity of earthquakes, as well as map their frequency much more accurately.

Charles Richter died in Pasadena on September 30, 1985.

◆◆◆

83

Wilhelm Conrad Roentgen

(1845-1923)

German physicist Wilhelm Conrad Roentgen won the first Nobel Prize in Physics for his discovery of the remarkable rays subsequently named after him.

Wilhelm Conrad Roentgen was born on March 27, 1845, at Lennep in the Lower Rhine, Province of Germany.

When he was three years old, his family moved to the Netherlands, where he went to the Institute of Martinus Herman van Doorn, a boarding school. He was especially apt at making mechanical contrivances, a characteristic which remained with him also in later life.

He Studied physics at University of Utrecht in 1865.

In 1869 he got his Ph.D. from the University of Zurich, was appointed assistant to Kundt and went with him to Würzburg in the same year, and three years later to Strasbourg.

In 1874 he was Lecturer at Strasbourg University and in 1875 Professor in the Academy of Agriculture at Hohenheim in Wurtemberg.

In 1876 he returned to Strasbourg as Professor of Physics, but three years later he accepted the invitation to the Chair of Physics in the University of Giessen in Germany, where he remained until 1888, when he became professor of physics and director of the Physical Institute at the University of Würzburg..

In 1900 he accepted the chair of physics in the University of Munich. Here he remained for the rest of his life.

Roentgen's first work was published in 1870, dealing with the specific heats of gases, followed a few years later by a paper on the thermal conductivity of crystals. He studied the electrical and other characteristics of quartz; the influence of pressure on the refractive indices of various fluids; the modification of the planes of polarised light by electromagnetic influences; the variations in the functions of the temperature and the compressibility of water and other fluids; the phenomena accompanying the spreading of oil drops on water.

Roentgen's name, however, is chiefly associated with his discovery of the rays that he called X-rays. In 1895 he was studying the phenomena accompanying the passage of an electric current through a gas of extremely low pressure. His work on cathode rays led him, however, to the discovery of a new and different kind of rays.

During experiments he found that objects of different thicknesses interposed in the path of the rays showed variable transparency to them when recorded on a photographic plate. When he immobilised for some moments the hand of his wife in the path of the rays over a photographic plate, he observed after development of the plate an image of his wife's hand which showed the shadows thrown by the bones of her hand and that of a ring she was wearing, surrounded by the penumbra of the flesh, which was more permeable to the rays and therefore threw a fainter shadow. This was the first 'roentgenogram' ever taken. In further experiments, he showed that the new rays are produced by the impact of cathode rays on a material object. Because their nature was then unknown, he gave them the name X-rays.

His fame for the discovery of X rays overshadowed his important studies of gases and crystalline substances, conducted between 1876 and 1895.

Roentgen died in 1923.

◆◆◆

84

Sir Ronald Ross

(1857-1932)

Sir Ronald Ross, English physician, studied malaria in India as a member (1881–99) of the Indian Medical Service, was professor of tropical medicine at University College, Liverpool, from 1902, and directed the Ross Institute and Hospital for Tropical Diseases, London, from 1926. In 1898 he demonstrated the malarial parasite (Plasmodium) in the stomach of the Anopheles mosquito; in W Africa he discovered the mosquito that transmits African fever. He received the 1902 Nobel Prize in Physiology or Medicine for his work on malaria and was knighted in 1911.

Ronald Ross was born at Almora in India in 1857.

Ross lived in India until he was eight when he was sent away to boarding school in Southampton, England. At school he seemed to have been a dreamy imaginative boy whose main interest was in writing poetry, painting and composing music.

In 1874 he became a medical student at St Bartholomew's Hospital in London. In 1879 he just managed to pass his Royal College of Surgeons exam — after three days cramming. This meant that he could only practice as a ship's surgeon, which he did for a couple of years until he passed an exam for the Society of Apothecaries.

In 1881 Ross could join the British-Indian army medical services and eleven years later he began investigating the transmission and control of malaria.

When Ross returned to India as part of the British-Indian medical services he was sent to Madras where he found that a large part of his work was treating soldiers, ill with malaria. The treatment was with quinine which was quite successful, but many died because they failed to get treatment.

While he was posted in India, Ross returned to England a number of times and in 1889, on leave in England he took a course in bacteriology. This was a new discipline and gave him an opportunity to use a microscope.

In 1894-95 Ross returned to England again for a long holiday and while there he discussed his theories with Dr Patrick Manson, a specialist in tropical diseases. They also discussed the work of Laveran, a French doctor who had recently identified parasites called Plasmodium in the blood of people from North Africa who had malaria. Dr Manson and Ross then examined some tiny drops of blood taken from sailors who had come from Africa through a microscope. These showed the Plasmodium parasite infecting the red blood cells.

When, in 1895 Ross returned to India he had an increased interest in establishing the link between mosquitoes and malaria and carried out a series of experiments to prove this theory.

One of the difficulties Ross faced was that there were many different sorts of mosquitoes and it was possible only one type carried the parasite. Things were to improve in 1898 when he was posted to Calcutta where a laboratory was made available to him. While there, he read the work of an American called MacCallum who had identified the Plasmodium parasite in infected birds. He decided to follow this line. He took mosquitoes fed on infected birds and fed them on uninfected birds. The uninfected birds became infected.

Reporting back to Manson on the 25 June Ross wrote that he had found 'germinal rods', in the stomach lining of the mosquito. By 29 June he had located them in the blood cavity and on the 4 July he found them in the salivary glands. The complicated lifecycle of the plasmodium parasite had been uncovered. The parasite bred in the stomach of the female mosquito, travelled through the bloodstream to the salivary glands and was injected into the victim with the saliva when the mosquito bit through the skin.

That month Manson declared Ross's work to the BMA.

In 1899 Ross decided to return to England. Manson had arranged a post for him at the Liverpool School of Tropical Medicine and Ross became their first lecturer in tropical disease. He remained involved with the Liverpool School of Tropical Medicine from 1899 to 1912, during which time he was awarded the Nobel Prize for Medicine and in 1911 received a knighthood.

By 1912, however, Ross had become so disillusioned with his pay and conditions that he moved to London to improve his situation. While in London he saw the founding of the Ross Institute and Hospital for Tropical Diseases at Putney.

Ross died on 16 September 1932 at the Ross Institute after a long illness and was buried next to his wife at Putney Vale Cemetery.

◆◆◆

85

Ernest Rutherford

(1871-1937)

Ernest Rutherford was a New Zealand-born British chemist responsible for a remarkable series of discoveries in the fields of radioactivity and nuclear physics. He discovered alpha and beta rays, set forth the laws of radioactive decay, and identified alpha particles as helium nuclei. Most important, he postulated the nuclear structure of the atom and thereby pioneered the Rutherford model of the atom, through his discovery of Rutherford scattering with his gold foil experiment. He was awarded the Nobel Prize in Chemistry in 1908.

Ernest Rutherford was born on 30 August 1871 in Nelson, New Zealand.

Rutherford completed a degree at the University of New Zealand and began teaching unruly schoolboys.

In 1894 he won a scholarship to Cambridge University where he became J. J. Thomson's first graduate student at the Cavendish Laboratory. There he began experimenting with the transmission of radio waves, went on to join Thomson's ongoing investigation of the conduction of electricity through gases, and then turned to the field of radioactivity just opened up by Henri Becquerel and Pierre and Marie Curie.

In 1898 he became Professor of Physics at McGill University in Montreal, Canada. There, working with chemist Frederick Soddy, he investigated the newly-discovered phenomenon of radioactivity. Rutherford and Soddy proposed that radioactivity results from the disintegration of atoms.

At Manchester University he collaborated with Hans Geiger (of Geiger counter fame), Niels Bohr (whose model of atomic structure succeeded Rutherford's), and H. G. J. Moseley (who obtained experimental evidence for atomic numbers). During World War I, this Manchester research group was largely dispersed, and Rutherford turned to solving problems connected with submarine detection.

In 1908, he was awarded the Nobel Prize in Chemistry.

In 1914 he was knighted, but the war interrupted his work. He helped to develop methods of dealing with the new menace of submarine warfare, as well as studying underwater acoustics.

In 1917 he returned to physics and a long series of experiments in which he discovered that the nuclei of certain light elements, such as nitrogen, could be 'disintegrated' by the impact of energetic alpha particles coming from some radioactive source, and that during this process fast protons were emitted. This was the first artificially induced nuclear reaction. Rutherford had virtually created a new discipline, that of nuclear physics.

After the war he succeeded J. J. Thomson in the Cavendish Professorship at Cambridge and again gathered a vigorous research group, including James Chadwick, the discoverer of the neutron.

Like his mentor Thomson, Rutherford garnered many honours. He received the Nobel Prize in chemistry for 1908; he was made a knight, then a peer with a seat in the House of Lords.

From 1925 to 1930 he was president of the Royal Society (to which he had been elected in 1903).

1931 he was awarded a life peerage. He died on 19 October 1937, and for the ultimate honor he was buried in Westminster Abbey.

In 1997, the rutherford, a unit of radioactivity, was named in his honour.

◆◆◆

86

Jonas Edward Salk

(1914-1995)

Jonas Edward Salk was an American biologist and physician best known for the research and development of a killed-virus polio vaccine, the eponymous Salk vaccine. He proposed a novel "therapeutic vaccine" approach to control AIDS. He established the Salk Institute for Biological Studies, one of the preeminent biomedical research centers in the world today. He set the stage for the development of psychoneuroi-mmunology.

Jonas Edward Salk was born on October 28, 1914 in New York City.

He became interested in biology and chemistry and decided to go into research. He went to New York University medical school for training. There in 1938 he began working with microbiologist Thomas Francis, Jr., who was looking for an influenza vaccine. They developed one that was used in the armed forces during World War II. He graduated from New York University School of Medicine in 1938.

In 1942, he went to the University of Michigan on a research fellowship and soon advanced to the position of assistant professor of epidemiology (the study of the causes and control of epidemics).

Salk began teaching at the University of Pittsburgh in 1947 where he continued his research. He became the head of the Virus Research Lab at the University of Pittsburgh. He worked on improving the flu vaccine and began to study poliovirus with hopes of creating a vaccine against that disease, as well. He applied findings from many other scientists to this problem. From some he found a way to produce large quantities of the virus; from others a way to kill the virus with formaldehyde so that it remained intact enough to cause a response in humans.

In 1952 he first inoculated volunteers, including himself, his wife, and their three sons, with a polio vaccine made from this killed virus. Everyone who received the test vaccine began producing antibodies to the disease, yet no one became ill. The vaccine seemed safe and effective.

The following year he published the results in the *Journal of the American Medical Association*, and nationwide testing was carried out. In 1953 he announced the development of a trial vaccine for Polio (poliomyelitis). His vaccine was composed of 'killed' polio virus, which retained the ability to immunise without the risk of infecting the patient. Mass trials held in 1953 on 1,830,000 children proved the vaccine was safe and effective. The success of the vaccination effort won Jonas Salk unsought fame. He also made significant contributions to our understanding of influenza and other infectious diseases.

He received many honours, including a Congressional gold medal for his great achievement in the field of medicine.

Salk established the Institute for Biological Studies in La Jolla, California in 1963.

He left his position at University of Pittsburgh in 1964 to dedicate full-time to his institute, and the study of infectious diseases.

He was director of the Salk Institute until his death on June 23, 1995. He was 80 years old.

◆◆◆

87

Frederick Sanger

(1918-1983)

Fredrick Sanger is an English biochemist and twice a Nobel laureate in chemistry. He is the fourth (and only living) person to have been awarded two Nobel Prizes.

Fredrick Sanger was born on August 13, 1918, in Rendcomble, Gloucestershire, United Kingdom.

From 1932 to 1936, he attended the Bryanston School in Dorest, England.

He received both his B.A. and his Ph. D. from Cambridge University (in 1939 and 1943 respectively).

He continued his research at the university. From 1962 until his retirement in 1983, and he served as head of the Protein and Nucleic Acid Chemistry Division at the MRC's Labortory of Molecular Biology in Cambridge.

In 1951 Sanger was awarded the Corday-Morgan Medal of the Chemical Society. In 1954 he was elected a Fellow of the Royal Society and a Fellow of King's College, Cambridge; and in 1958 he was elected a Foreign Honorary Member of the American Academy of Arts and Sciences.

While at Cambridge University in England he developed a new method for sequencing amino acids in proteins, which he used to identify the complete sequence of insulin. For this he was awarded his first Nobel Prize in chemistry in 1958. His work enabled chemists to synthesize insulin artificially and generally stimulated research in protein structure.

After this success, in 1961 Sanger moved to the MRC Laboratory of Molecular Biology, where he became head of the division of protein chemistry. His colleagues' interest in nucleic acids inspireed him to turn his interest in sequencing to the research of nucleic acids.

In 1977 Sanger developed a sequencing method, called the 'dideoxy' method, with which he determined the entire sequence of a bacterial virus called phi-X174. This was the first time a complete sequence of a DNA molecule had been established. For this achievement he was awarded the 1980 Nobel Prize in chemistry, shared jointly with Walter Gilbert of Harvard University who had concurrently developed an alternative DNA sequencing method. In fact, he is the only person to have won a Nobel Prize in chemistry twice, and is only one of four people ever to have won a Nobel Prize more than once.

He received the Royal Society's Royal Medal in 1969, and the Copely Medal in 1977. He was named a Commander of the Order of the British Empire in 1963. He received the William Bate Hardy Prize of the Cambridge Philosophical Society in 1976. In 1979, he won the Albert Lasker Basic Medical Research Award.

Sanger retired from research in 1983.

◆◆◆

88

Erwin Schrödinger

(1887-1961)

Erwin Rudolf Josef Alexander Schröndinger, an Austrian physicist, achieved fame for his contributions to quantum mechanics, especially the Schrodinger equation, for which he won the Nobel Prize in 1933. He proposed the Schrödinger's Cat thought experiment.

Schrödinger was born on August 12, 1887, in Vienna.

In 1906 he entered the University of Vienna, where he was most stimulated by the experimental physicist Franz Exner and the theoretical physicist Fritz Hasenöhrl. After he completed his doctoral degree in 1910, he remained as an assistant to Exner. In that capacity he explored various problems, many in solid-state physics.

In 1914 Schröndinger became privatdozent at Vienna but almost immediately found himself serving as an artillery officer in Italy.

In 1920, he went to the University of Jena as an assistant to Max Wien. Within next year he was called, first as associate professor to the Technische Hochschule in Stuttgart, then as full professor to the University of Breslau, and finally as full professor to the University of Zurich. His years at Zurich (1921-1927) were, scientifically speaking, the most productive in his career.

The non-relativistic wave equation that Schrödinger assumed to govern the behaviour of the electron in the hydrogen atoms was of course the equation now university known as the Schröndinger Wave Equation, the fundamental equation of wave mechanics. The capstone of his achievements was his proof of the logical equivalence of wave mechanics and 'matrix mechanics', the latter discovered almost simultaneously by Werner Heisenberg in 1926.

In 1927 Schröndinger became Max Planck's successor at the University of Berlin, where he remained until the political events of 1933. That year he received the Nobel Prize in physics, sharing it with Paul Dirac.

Schröndinger was a fellow at Oxford University from 1933 to 1936, when he accepted a professorship at the Unversity of Graz.

He was professor at the University of Vienna (1957-61)

He went to Dublin in 1939 as director of the institute's Schoold of Theoretical Physics.

He carried out studies on relativity, cosmology, the unified field theory, meson physics, counter (detector) statistics, and statistical mechanics.

By the time he left Dublin in 1956 for Vienna (where a special chair in theoretical physics was created for him), his health was badly damaged and his productive life in physics was over.

Schrödinger died in Vienna on January 4, 1961.

89

Sir James Young Simpson

(1811-1870)

Sir James Young Simpson was a Scottish obstetrician. He discovered the anaesthetic properties of chloroform and successfully introduced it for general medical use. He also introduced iron wire sutures, the use of pressure to stop bleeding, and Simpson forceps long obstetrical.

James Simpson was born on 7 June 1811 in Bathgate, Linlithgowshire, Scotland.

He received his M.D. from the University of Edinburgh, where he became professor of obstetrics.

At the age of fourteen James Simpson left Bathgate and was enrolled as a student in the art classes of Edinburgh University.

In 1827 he began his medical studies, and determined to be a doctor. In 1830 he passed his final examination with honours, and in 1831, when only just out of his teens, he was made a member of the Royal College of Surgeons at Edinburgh.

In 1835 he settled down to equire an Edinburgh practice, and set up his plate in Heriot Row, Stockbridge. Before the end of January 1840, Dr. Simpson had become Professor Simpson.

He soon became Scotland's leading obstetrician, acquiring a sizable practice through demonstrated ability and remarkable personality. During his lifetime, he received many honours, including a baronetcy (1866); the Freedom of the City of Edinburgh; and an honorary degree from Oxford University.

In November of 1847 (the same year he was apointed physician to the Queen in Scotland), he began to employ chloroform in obstetrics and labour, but only after a preliminary test that involved inhaling it experimentally himself, as also did his assistants Mathews Duncan and George Keith. Simpson immediately found himself embroiled with Calvinists who were opposed to the use of any anaesthetic in childbirth. It was not until 1853, when Queen Victoria accepted the use of chloroform for the birth of her son that criticism of Simpson began to subside.

In 1858, Simpson introduced iron wire, sutures, between 1850 and 1864, he pioneered the use of long obstetric forceps. Other contributions in gynecology and obstetrics included the use of uterine sound (1843), the sponge tent, dilatation of the cervix uteri in diagnosis, Simpson's pains in uterine cancer (1863), and inversion in deformed pelvis. He wrote important memoirs on foetal pathology and hermaphroditism, and made contributions in the fields of archeology and medical history (particularly on leprosy in Scotland; 1841 to 1842). He introduced village of pavilion hospitals in Scotland.

Simpson died at his home in Edinburgh on May 6, 1870.

◆◆◆

90

Percy Lebaron Spencer

(1894-1970)

Percy Lebaron Spencer was an American engineer and inventor who became known as the inventor of the microwave oven.

Spencer was born in Howland, Maine in 1894.

He was raised by an impoverished aunt and uncle, and had little formal schooling. In his teens he was intrigued by the burgeoning use of electric power and worked as an electric installer, wiring businesses with power. He never graduated from a traditional school but his brains carried him through life and never failed him.

He then joined the Navy, where he was sent to radio school, and after being discharged he worked for Wireless Specialty Apparatus Company, a major manufacturer of commercial and military radio equipment that was eventually absorbed into RCA.

He joined Raytheon in the 1920s, and quickly became the company's expert on tube design. While working for the Raytheon Company, he discovered a more efficient way to manufacture magnetrons.

In 1941, magnetrons were being produced at a rate of 17 per day. Spencer set out to create a simpler magnetron that could be mass produced. The result was a magnetron that replaced precision copper bars with lamina and replaced soldered internal wires with a simple solid ring. These improvements and others allowed for the faster production of 2,600 magnetrons per day. During World War II he oversaw the company's exponential increase in manufacturing tubes for military applications, and the mass production of magnetrons (which power radar equipment), which proved of immeasurable value to allied forces in winning that war.

His discovery of microwave cooking was utterly accidental. In a Raytheon laboratory in 1946, he noticed that he felt a tingling when he stood near a magnetron. Around the same time, he realised that his chocolate candy bar was melting. As he noted these strange and peculiar happenings, he also recognised that both were a result of where he chose to stand. He brought in raw popcorn, which started popping when he placed it near the magnetron. He then built a rudimentary metal box with a magnetron in it — the first microwave oven — and used it to reheat his lunches. From the experiment conducted at Raytheon, the microwave was developed. The first oven was basically developed for the use in commercial settings like restaurants and ocean vessels or railroad cars. These ovens weighed around seven hundred and fifty pounds.

After he wrote a report on his findings, Raytheon patented "high frequency dielectric heating apparatus" in 1946, and began selling microwave ovens for industrial use (more than five feet tall, each oven weighed about 750 pounds) in 1954. Raytheon subsidiary Amana began selling household 'RadarRange' ovens in 1967.

For his invention, Spencer received no royalties, but he was paid a one-time, two-dollar gratuity from Raytheon — the same token payment the company made to all inventors on its payroll at that time, for company patents.

He left behind a lifetime of accomplishments. During his time at Raytheon, not only did he invent the microwave but he also held the position of Senior Vice-President of Raytheon.

Percy L. Spencer secured over one hundred patents during his lifetime

Spencer died in 1970.

◆◆◆

91

Sushruta

(c.380-c.450)

Sushruta is the greatest surgeon in Indian history. His work Sushruta Samhita, one of the most brilliant gems in Indian medical literature, contains information on surgical practices of ancient Indian, several centuries before Christ. It has medical knowledge, relevant even today. He is recognised as the father of Indian surgery.

Born in the sixth century B.C., Sushruta was a descendant of the Vedic sage Vishwamitra.

He learnt surgery and medicine at the feet of Divodasa Dhanvantari in his hermitage at Varanasi. Later, he became an authority in not only surgery but other branches of medicine.

He was the first physician to advocate what is today known as the 'caesarean' operation. He was also expert in removing urinary stones, locating and treating fractures and doing eye operations for cataract.

Several centuries before Joseph Lister, he put forth the concept of asepsis. His suggestion to give wine to patients about to be operated upon makes him also the father of anaesthesia.

In his treatise, Sushruta lists 101 types of instruments. His Samdamsa yantras are the first forms of the modren surgeon's spring forceps and dissection and dressing forceps. In fact, his system of naming surgical tools after the animals or birds they resemble in shape, for example crocodile forceps, hawkbill forceps, is adopted even today.

In addition to classifying worms that infect the human body, leeches for bloodletting, medicinal herbs, alkalis and metals, Sushruta gave a vague classification of animals.

He has mentioned various methods including sliding graft, rotation graft and pedicle graft. Nasal repair or rhinoplasty has been described in greater detail, which to this day has stood the test of time and is mentioned as the Indian method of rhinoplasty in the books of plastic surgery. Lastly, labioplasty too has received his attention. In short, all the principles of plastic surgery, viz., accuracy, precision, economy, haemostasis and perfection, find an important place in Sushruta's writings on this subject.

It was through the efforts of Sushruta that surgery achieved a leading position in general medical training.

◆◆◆

92

Leon Philippe Teisserenc De Bort

(c.380-c.450)

Teisserenc de Bort, a French meteorologist, pioneered the use of unmanned instrumented balloons and was the first to identify the region in the atmosphere around 8-17 kilometres of height where the lapse rate reaches zero, known today as the tropopause.

Léon Phillipe Teisserenc de Bort was born on November 5, 1855 in Paris.

He began his scientific career in 1880, when he entered the meteorological department of the Bureau Central Meteorologique in Paris under E. E. W. Mascart. He worked as chief meteorologist from 1892 until 1896, when he opened his own meteorological observatory at Trappes, near Versailles. Here he carried out investigations on clouds and the problems of the upper air.

In 1883, 1885 and 1887 he made journeys to N. Africa to study geology and terrestrial magnetism, and during this period published some important charts of the distribution of pressure at a height of 4,000 metres.

In 1898 he published an important paper in *Cornptes Rendus* detailing his researches by means of balloons into the constitution of the atmosphere.

In 1902 he discovered the stratosphere while putting forward his conclusions on the atmosphere. His discovery of the so-called isothermal layer, or stratosphere as it is now generally called, will always stand out as one of the most important events in the study of the upper atmosphere.

Early balloonists had established that temperature decreased with height by about 0.6°C per 330 feet (100 m). A pioneer in using unmanned instrumented balloons Teisserenc de Bort found that above an altitude of 7 miles (11 km) temperature ceased to fall and sometimes increased slightly. He named this upper part of the atmosphere the stratosphere, because he thought that the different gases would lie in distinct strata as, without temperature differentials, there would be no mechanism to disturb them. The lower part of the atmosphere he named the troposphere as here, with abundant temperature differentials, constant change and mingling of atmospheric gases occurred.

The phenomenon was explained by E. Gold in 1909 by reference to cooling of rising air in the troposphere and the absence of convection currents in the stratosphere.

He also carried out investigations in Sweden and over the Zuider Zee, the Mediterranean and the tropical region of the Atlantic, and fitted out a special vessel in order to study the currents above the trade-winds.

He was elected a fellow of the Royal Meteorological Society in 1903, honorary member in 1909, and was awarded the Symons gold medal of the society in 1908. He collaborated with Hugo Hildebrandsson in *Les bases de la meteorologie dynamique* (1907).

Teisserenc de Bort died on January 2, 1913 in Cannes.

93

Sir Joseph John Thomson

(1856-1940)

Sir J. J. Thomson was a British physicist who discovered the electron which resulted in the development of Electronics, a branch of Physics.

Joseph John Thomson was born on December 18, 1856 near Manchester, England.

Thomson attended Owens College in Manchester, where his professor of mathematics encouraged him to apply for a scholarship at Trinity College. He won the scholarship, and in 1880 finished second in his class in mathematics. Trinity gave him a fellowship and he stayed on there, trying to craft mathematical models that would reveal the nature of atoms and electromagnetic forces. He became a mathematical physicist there.

In 1884 he was named to the prestigious Cavendish Professorship of Experimental Physics at Cambridge. He had a genius for designing apparatus and diagnosing its problems. He was a good lecturer, encouraged his students, and devoted considerable attention to the wider problems of science teaching at university and secondary levels.

Thomson discovered the electron in a series of experiments designed to study the nature of electric discharge in a high-vacuum cathode-ray tube. He interpreted the deflection of the rays by electrically charged plates and magnets as evidence of 'bodies much smaller than atoms' that he calculated as having a very large value for the charge to mass ratio. Later he estimated the value of the charge itself.

In 1904 he suggested a model of the atom as a sphere of positive matter in which electrons are positioned by electrostatic forces. His efforts to estimate the number of electrons in an atom from measurements of the scattering of light, X, beta, and gamma rays initiated the research trajectory along which his student Ernest Rutherford moved.

Thomson's last important experimental programme focused on determining the nature of positively charged particles. Here his techniques led to the development of the mass spectroscope, an instrument perfected by his assistant, Francis Aston, for which Aston received the Nobel Prize in 1922.

Thomson received the Nobel Prize in physics in 1906 for his researches into the discharge of electricity in gases, and a knighthood in 1908. He also had the great pleasure of seeing several of his close associates receive their own Nobel prizes.

He was elected Fellow of the Royal Society in 1884 and was President during 1916-1920; he received the Royal and Hughes Medals in 1894 and 1902, and the Copley Medal in 1914. He was awarded the Hodgkins Medal (Smithsonian Institute, Washington) in 1902; the Franklin Medal and Scott Medal (Philadelphia), 1923; the Mascart Medal (Paris), 1927; the Dalton Medal (Manchester), 1931; and the Faraday Medal (Institute of Civil Engineers) in 1938.

He was President of the British Association in 1909 and he held honorary doctorate degrees from the Universities of Oxford, Dublin, London, Victoria, Columbia, Cambridge, Durham, Birmingham, Göttingen, Leeds, Oslo, Sorbonne, Edinburgh, Reading, Princeton, Glasgow, Johns Hopkins, Aberdeen, Athens, Cracow and Philadelphia.

In 1918 he was chosen Master of his old college, Trinity, and the next year he resigned the Cavendish Professorship.

He died on August 30, 1940.

◆◆◆

94

Tim Berners-Lee

(1955-)

Tim Berners-Lee, a British computer whiz, radically changed the history of computing and communication when he invented the World Wide Web in 1989.

Tim Berners-Lee was born in London on 8 June 1955.

Berners-Lee's education included Emanuel School in Wandsworth, and later Queen's College, Oxford. Tim graduated from the Queen's College at Oxford University, England, in 1976. At Oxford he majored in physics and built his own computer out of spare parts consisting of a soldering iron, TTL gates, an M6800 processor and an old television.

Berners-Lee was also caught hacking during his stay at Oxford and banned from using the university's computer.

After graduating from Oxford in 1976, he worked on various programming projects before taking a position as a consultant/ software engineer for CERN, the European particle physics laboratory in Geneva, Switzerland, in 1980.

He spent two years with Plessey Telecommunications Ltd in Dorset, a major UK Telecom equipment manufacturer, working on distributed transaction systems, message relays, and bar code technology.

In 1978 Tim left Plessey to join D.G Nash Ltd in Dorset, UK, where he wrote among other things typesetting software for intelligent printers, and a multitasking operating system.

Berners-Lee moved on to other projects, in 1984 he returned to CERN. He took up a fellowship at CERN. A year and a half spent as an independent consultant included a six month stint as consultant software engineer at CERN, the European Particle Physics Laboratory in Geneva, Switzerland. It was here that he developed the first prototype of the 'World Wide Web'. Called 'Enquire', the programme was designed to help him keep track of the vast web of researchers and projects connected with CERN. The programme was never released for public use. Whilst there, he wrote for his own private use his first programme for storing information including using random associations. Never published, this programme formed the conceptual basis for the future development of the World Wide Web.

From 1981 until 1984, Tim worked at John Poole's Image Computer Systems Ltd., with technical design responsibility. Work here included real time control firmware, graphics and communications software, and a generic macro language.

Among other things, he worked on FASTBUS system software and designed a heterogeneous remote procedure call system.

In 1989, he proposed a global hypertext project, to be known as the 'World Wide Web'. Based on the earlier Enquire work, it was designed to allow people to work together by combining their knowledge in a web of hypertext documents. He wrote the first 'World Wide Web' server, 'httpd', and the first client, 'World Wide Web' a what-you-see-is-what-you-get hypertext browser/ editor which ran in the Next Step environment. This work was started in October, 1990, and the programme 'World Wide Web' first made available within CERN in December, and on the Internet at large in the summer of 1991.

Drawing on the 1945 work of Vannevar Bush as well as later work by Ted Nelson and Doug Engelbart, he wrote the Hypertext Transfer Protocol (HTTP) or language that computers would use to communicate hypertext documents via the Internet. He also worked out a scheme for locating the documents: each document would be assigned a Universal Resource Identifier, or URI, essentially its own unique address (now called a URL, or Uniform Resource Locator).

Through 1991 and 1993, Tim continued working on the design of the Web, coordinating feedback from users across the Internet. His initial specifications of URLs, HTTP and HTML were refined and discussed in larger circles as the Web technology spread.

In 1994, he joined the Laboratory for Computer Science (LCS) at the Massachusetts Institute of Technology (MIT).

In 1999, he became the first holder of the 3Com Founders chair. A Distinguished Fellow of the British Computer Society and Honorary Fellow of the Institute of Electrical and Electronics Engineers, he is both a member of the American Academy of Arts and Sciences, and a Fellow of the British Royal Society.

He is Director of the World Wide Web Consortium which coordinates Web development worldwide, with teams at MIT, at INRIA in France, and at Keio University in Japan.

◆◆◆

95

Evangelista Torricelli

(1608-1647)

Evangelista Torricelli was an Italian scientist and mathematician who was the first man to create a sustained vacuum and to discover the principle of a barometer. He also achieved some important results in the development of the calculus.

Evangelista Torricelli was born at Faenza, Italy on 15 October 1608.

He entered a Jesuit College in 1624 and studied mathematics and philosophy there until 1626.

As well as being taught mathematics, mechanics, hydraulics and astronomy, Torricelli became a secretary to his uncle and held this post from 1626 to 1632.

Torricelli was fascinated by astronomy and was a strong supporter of Galileo. After Galileo's trial in 1633, Torricelli realised that he would be on dangerous ground were he to continue with his interests in the Copernican theory, so he deliberately shifted his attention onto mathematical areas which seemed less controversial. During the next nine years he served as secretary to Giovanni Ciampoli, a friend of Galileo.

He only had a few months with Galileo, however, before that famous scientist died in January 1642. Torricelli was appointed to succeed Galileo as the court mathematician to Grand Duke Ferdinando II of Tuscany. He held this post until his death living in the ducal palace in Florence.

By 1641 he had proved a number of impressive results using the methods which he would publish three years later. He examined the three dimensional figures obtained by rotating a regular polygon about an axis of symmetry. He also computed the area and centre of gravity of the cycloid. His most remarkable results, however, resulted from his extension of Cavalieri's method of indivisibles to cover curved indivisibles. With these tools he showed that rotating the unlimited area of a rectangular hyperbola between the y-axis and a fixed point on the curve, resulted in a finite volume when rotated round the y-axis.

Torricelli published his work in three parts as *Opera Geometrica* in 1644. He also proved that the flow of liquid through an opening is proportional to the square root of the height of the liquid, a result now known as Torricelli's theorem. This has led to some suggesting that this result makes him the founder of hydrodynamics.

Also in *De motu gravium* Torricelli studied projectile motion. He developed Galileo's ideas on the parabolic trajectory of projectiles launched horizontally, giving a theory for projectiles launched at any angle. He also gave numerical tables which would help gunners find the correct elevation of their guns to give the required range.

Torricelli also had great skill as a maker of instruments. He was a skilled lens grinder, making excellent telescopes and small, short focus, simple microscopes, techniques learnt during the time he lived with Galileo.

Torricelli was the first person to create a sustained vacuum and to discover the principle of a barometer. In 1643 he proposed an experiment, later performed by his colleague Vincenzo Viviani, that demonstrated that atmospheric pressure determines the height to which a fluid will rise in a tube inverted over the same liquid.

Torricelli contracted typhoid in October 1647 died in Florence a few days later at the young age of 39 while in his prime as a research mathematician and scientist.

◆◆◆

96

Alessandro Giuseppe Volta

(1745-1827)

Alessandro Volta, an Italian physicist, is known for the development of the first electric cell in 1800.

Count Alessandro Giuseppe Antonio Anastasio Volta was born in Como, Lombardy, on February 18, 1745.

His young childhood did not show the makings of a prodigy. However, at the age of seven when his father died, he was at the level of other children and then began to march ahead. By the age of fourteen, he made up his mind to be a physicist.

Volta became fascinated with the phenomenon of the age, electricity. In 1774, he was appointed professor of physics in the Como high school and the next year he invented electrophorous, a charge-accumulating machine. The electrophorous was a device based on static electricity. It consisted of one metal plate covered with ebonite and a second metal plate with an insulated handle. The ebonite-covered plate is rubbed and given a negative electric charge. If the plate with a handle is placed over it, a positive electric charge is attracted to the lower surface, a negative charge repelled to the upper. The upper negative charge is built up in the plate with the handle. This sort of charge-accumulating machine replaced the Leyden Jar and is the basis of the electrical condensers still used today. His fame spread as result.

The Voltaic pile was Volta's life accomplishment. Initially, he used bowls of salt solution that were connected by means of arcs of metal dipping from one bowl into the next, one end of the arc being copper and the other tin or zinc. He made matters more compact and less watery by using small round plates of copper and zinc, plus discs of cardboard moistened in salt solution. Starting with copper at the bottom, the discs, reading upward, were in the pattern copper, zinc, cardboard. If a wire was attached to the top and bottom of this Voltaic pile, an electric current would pass through it if the circuit was closed.

The voltaic pile was the first electric battery, and it shortly led to its practical application by William Nicholson and the work of Davy, as well as, being the progenitor of modern day batteries.

In 1778, Volta was the first to isolate the compound methane, a major constituent of natural gas.

Further, in 1779, he received a professorial appointment at the University of Pavia, where he continued his work with electricity. He invented other gadgets involving static electricity and received the Copley medal of the Royal Society, where he was elected to membership, in 1791.

The major feat of his life involved not static electricity, but dynamic electricity — the electric current. Following the experiments of Galvani, who was a friend of his and sent copies of his papers on the subject, Volta attacked the question of whether the electric current resulting when muscle was in contact with two different metals arose from the tissue or from the metals.

To check this he decided in 1794 to make use of the metals alone, without the tissue. He found at once that an electric current resulted and maintained that it therefore had nothing to do with life or tissue. This sparked a controversy between the two Italians with the German Humboldt, the chief of Galvani's supporters, and the Frenchman Coulomb, the chief of Volta's. The weight of the evidence leaned more and more heavily toward Volta, and Galvani died embittered.

In 1800 Volta virtually clinched the victory by constructing a device that would produce a large flow of electricity. His device was an 'electric battery' — the first in history. The invention of the battery lifted Volta's fame to its pinnacle.

He was called to France by Napoleon in 1801 for a kind of 'command performance' of his experiments. He received many medals and decorations, including the Legion of Honor, and was even made a count and, in 1810, a senator of the kingdom of Lombardy

After Napoleon fell and Austria became dominant in Italy once more, Volta continued to excel and to receive posts of high honour. He received his greatest honour, however, at the hands of no ruler, but of his fellow scientists. The unit of electromotive force — the driving force that moves the electric current — is now called the 'volt' in his honour and was adopted internationally in 1881.

He died on 5 March 1827.

◆◆◆

97

Max Theodor Felix Von Laue

(1879-1960)

Max Theodor Felix Von Laue was a German physicist who won the Nobel Prize in Physics in 1914 for his discovery of the diffraction of x-rays by crystals. This enabled scientists to study the structure of crystals and hence marked the origin of solid-state physics, an important field in the development of modern electronics. In addition to his scientific endeavors, he made valuable contributions in optics, crystallography, quantum theory, superconductivity and the theory of relativity.

Max Theodor Felix Von Laue was born on October 9, 1879, in Pfaffendorf, Germany.

In the early 1890s the young von Laue gained a passionate interest in physics that lasted until his death some 60 years later.

Von Laue studied mathematics, physics and chemistry at the University of Strassburg. This was followed by periods at the University of Göttingen and the University of Berlin, where he worked under Max Planck in the Institute of Theoretical Physics in Berlin. He was awarded a doctorate in mathematics and physics by the University of Berlin (1903) where he came under the influence of Max Planck, one of the greatest physicists of the 20th century.

In the fall of 1905 Planck offered von Laue a post at the Institute for Theoretical Physics. The four years during which he worked closely with Planck marked the beginning of his career as a creative scientist. An early and lifelong champion of the physical ideas of Albert Einstein, he began publishing papers on the theory of relativity in 1907.

In 1909 von Laue moved to the University of Munich where he was associated with yet another distinguished physicist, Arnold Sommerfield. He lectured on optics and thermodynamics at the University of Munich before becoming Professor of Physics at the University of Zurich. Continuing his interest in relativity at Munich, he prepared a 200-page monograph on the subject, the first such book to be published on Einstein's revolutionary theories. At Sommerfield's suggestion he began writing a treatise on wave optics. This undertaking led him to the famous work on x-ray analysis of the atomic structure of crystalline material.

The precise nature of x-radiation, discovered by W. C. Roentgen in 1895, had not yet been determined when von Laue initiated his study of x-rays. Von Laue's contribution was the insight that when using x-radiation the glass diffraction grating can be replaced by crystalline material. The regular spacing of the atoms in the crystal will affect x-rays penetrating it in the same way that the closely engraved lines of the grating affect light passing through. Von Laue, always the theoretician, did not actually make the necessary experiments, but those who did confirmed his predictions — x-rays diffracted by crystals yielded the expected interference patterns.

Von Laue's discovery, which Einstein hailed as one of the most beautiful in the history of physics, won him the Nobel Prize in 1914.

This pioneering work in x-ray crystallography opened the way for two quite different developments in physics, both of them of immense importance. First, it confirmed the electromagnetic nature of x-radiation and made it possible to determine the wave length of x-rays with great accuracy. Second, it gave physicists and chemists a new tool for investigating the atomic structure of matter. In the 1950s it was x-ray diffraction studies that enabled scientists to reveal the structure of the nucleic acids (DNA and RNA) and to establish the new discipline of molecular biology.

During the First World War Laue was engaged in military work. This included the development of high vacuum tubes used for German army's telephony and wireless communication.

After the war Laue became Director of the Institute of Theoretical Physics in Berlin. Subsequent research led him to refine his study of x-ray interference and to explore the phenomenon of super-conductivity whereby certain metals lose virtually all of their resistance to the flow of an electric current at temperatures approaching absolute zero (-273.16 C). He resigned from his post in 1943 in protest against the policies of the Nazi government.

Between the two world wars, von Laue became a leading statesman of German theoretical physics. He held high positions in academic scientific institutions and used his influence there to defend freedom of thought and expression in science.

After World War II von Laue laboured to revive German physics and bring it back into the world scientific community.

In 1951 he became director of the Max Planck Institute for Research in Physical Chemistry, a post he held until his retirement in 1958.

Two years later he lost his life in an automobile accident in Berlin on 23 April, 1960.

◆◆◆

98

James Dewey Watson

(1928-)

James Dewey Watson is an American molecular biologist, best known as one of the co-discoverers of the structure of DNA. Watson, Francis Crick, and Maurice Wilkins were awarded the 1962 Nobel Prize for their discoveries concerning the molecular structure of nucleic acids and its significance for information transfer in living material.

James Dewey Watson was born on April 6, 1928 in Chicago, Illinois.

He attended the Horace Mann Grammar School for eight years, then another two years at South Shore High School.

In 1947 Watson received a B. Sc. degree in Zoology and later Fellowship for graduate study in Zoology at the Indiana University in Bloomington. He acquired his Ph. D. degree in Zoology in 1950.

From 1950 to 1951 he worked in Copenhagen as a Merck Fellow of the National Research Council. While there he studied bacteria viruses, investigating the DNA of infecting viruses.

In 1951, Watson went to the Zoological Station at Naples and in late May met Maurice Wilkins. Wilkins showed him the x-ray diffraction pattern of crystalline DNA that he discovered. Watson then changed his research to structural chemistry of nucleic acid and proteins. He began working at Cavendish Laboratory at the University of Cambridge in October 1952, where he met Francis Crick. The two men shared an interest in discovering the DNA structure and began their efforts together. By 1953 they came up with the double helix model.

From 1953 to 1955 Watson was at the California Institute of Technology as Senior Research Fellow in Biology. Along with Alexander Rich, he studied RNA with x-ray diffraction. He worked again with Crick back at Cavendish from 1955 to 1956 publishing papers together on the principles of virus construction.

In 1956, Watson became Assistant Professor at Harvard Biology Department, Associate Professor in 1958 and then to Professor of Biology in 1961, a post he held until 1976. Here he researched the role of RNA in protein synthesis.

Watson, Crick and Wilkins shared the 1962 Nobel Prize in physiology or medicine.

Watson also received the following awards: John Collins Warren Prize of the Massachusetts General Hospital with Crick, 1959; Eli Lilly Award in Biochemisty, 1959; Lasker Award with Crick and Wilkins, 1960; Research Corporation Prize with Crick, 1962.

In 1968 Watson wrote *The Double Helix*, the story of Crick's and his discovery of the DNA structure. The book became an international best-seller.

While continuing his duties at Harvard, James Watson became Director of the Cold Spring Harbor Laboratory on Long Island.

From 1988 to 1992, he helped at the National Institute of Health, directing the Human Genome Project.

Watson left the Genome project in 1992, having seen it off to a successful start. He continued his work at Cold Spring Harbor Laboratory throughout this period, and in 1994 became President of that institution, and later served as its Chancellor.

Universities and governments around the world have honoured James Watson with honorary degrees and decorations, including the Presidential Medal of Freedom.

◆◆◆

99

James Watt

(1736-1819)

James Watt was a Scottish mathematician and engineer whose improvements to the steam engine were a key stage in the Industrial Revolution.

James Watt was born in Greenock, Scotland on January 19, 1736.

He was educated in the classics (Latin and Greek) and in mathematics at high school, but his father's workshop became the major source of his inspiration, where the young James spent his leisure time making models of machines, organs and other mechanical devices.

At the age of 17 Watt, who wanted to become an instrument maker, went to Glasgow and then to London, where he entered an apprenticeship. Finding London difficult for his health he returned to Glasgow to open his own shop for mathematical instruments in the university in 1757.

In 1764 Watt was given a steam engine for repairs. At the university he had met several scientists and had a good understanding of latent heat (heat stored in steam and released on condensation). The steam engine he was asked to repair was quite wasteful in that respect, since it lost all latent heat after the steam power was used to drive the piston.

A year later Watt had come up with his first major improvement of the steam engine: the separate condenser, where the latent heat is recovered and returned for use in the engine. He built his first improved steam engine in partnership with

John Roebuck, and in 1769 he took out his famous patent *A New Invented Method of Lessening the Consumption of Steam and Fuel in Fire Engines.*

The next years saw Watt employed as a surveyor, assisting in the building of canals. When John Roebuck went bankrupt in 1872, a share of Watt's patent was obtained by Matthew Boulton, an industrialist from Birmingham; so in 1774 Watt moved to Birmingham and, after his patent was extended by an act of Parliament, entered into a partnership with Boulton in 1775.

During the next five years Watt engines were installed in the mines of Cornwall, England. These engines were used for pumping water and used a piston with back-and-forth motion. Soon after 1780 Watt greatly helped the development of the embryonic steam engine into a viable and economic means of power generation. He realised that the Newcomen steam engine was wasting nearly three quarters of the steam energy in heating the piston and chamber. Watt developed a separate condenser chamber which significantly increased the efficiency. Further refinements (insulation of the steam cylinder, the double-acting engine, a counter, an indicator, and a throttle valve) made the steam engine his life's work.

In 1781 he invented the sun-and-planet gear, through which the reciprocating piston motion was converted into rotation. This opened new applications in corn and cotton mills and many other industries.

In 1782 he patented the double-action engine, in which steam is admitted alternately into both ends of the cylinder so that the piston is pushed in both directions.

In 1784 he invented the parallel motion, which allows the piston to always move along the axis of the cylinder.

In 1788 he invented the centrifugal or flyball governor, which allows automatic control of the engine's speed.

He introduced a unit called the horsepower to compare the power output of steam engines, his version of the unit being equivalent to 550 foot-pounds per second (about 745.7 watts).

Watt also invented several other things, not least a copying device for letters.

In 1790 he completed the 'Watt engine' by inventing the pressure gauge to monitor steam pressure.

Watt and Boulton were elected fellows of the Royal Society in 1785.

In 1806 he received a doctorate in law from the University of Glasgow. The French Académie des Sciences made him a foreign associate in 1814.

The SI unit of power, the watt, is named in his honour. So is, at least in part, Edinburgh's Heriot-Watt University.

He is also remembered by the Moonstones, two individual statues, and a statue of him, Boulton and Murdoch, by William Bloye, and a school named in his honour, all in Birmingham.

There are 4 colleges named after him in Scotland, James Watt College in Kilwinning and Greenock, and a campus in Largs.

Matthew Boulton's home, Soho House, is now a museum, commemorating the work of both men.

There are over 50 roads or streets named after him, in the UK.

◆◆◆

100

Alfered Wegener

(1880-1930)

Alfred Wegener was a German geologist, meteorologist and explorer. He is known for his theory of continental drift and his many expeditions to Greenland in which he measured the thickness of the ice. He is also known for his papers on lunar craters, in which he said that they were the result of impact rather than volcanic in origin.

Alfred Wegener was born in Berlin in 1880.

From an early age he took an interest in Greenland, and always walked, skated, and hiked as though training for an expedition. He studied in Germany and Austria, receiving his Ph.D. in astronomy. But no sooner did he finish his dissertation than he dropped astronomy to study meteorology, the new science of weather.

Wegener experimented with kites and balloons, and with his brother Kurt set a world record in an international balloon contest, flying 52 hours straight. That was in 1906, the year he made his first expedition to Greenland. He went as the official meteorologist on a two-year Danish expedition. When he returned he took up teaching meteorology at the University of Marburg, where he was a very popular lecturer.

In 1910, Wegener noticed the matching coastlines of the Atlantic continents — they looked on maps like they had once been fit together. He was not the first to notice this, but it was an idea that would never leave his thoughts. In 1911, he published a textbook on the thermodynamics of atmosphere, but at the same time he pursued his studies of the continents. He first spoke on the topic in January of 1912, where he put forth the idea of 'continental displacement' or what later was called continental drift.

Though he served in World War I and was wounded twice, he published his ideas in 1915. They constituted the first focused and rational argument for continental drift.

His book *The Origin of Continents and Oceans* contained extended accounts of his ideas on continental drift, and is the basis for the well established theory of plate tectonics. This work was one of the first to suggest continental drift and plate tectonics. He suggested that a supercontinent he called Pangaea had existed in the past, broke up starting 200 million years ago, and that the pieces 'drifted' to their present positions. He cited the fit of South America and Africa, ancient climate similarities, fossil evidence (such as the fern Glossopteris and mesosaurus), and similarity of rock structures.

In 1926 Wegener was finally offered a professorship in meteorology. In 1930 he sailed from Denmark as the leader of a major expedition to Greenland — his fourth and last. He celebrated his fiftieth birthday on November 1, but shortly afterwards the team got separated, and he was lost in a blizzard. His body was found halfway between the two camps.

◆◆◆

Other Books on

GENERAL BOOKS

1. Child Development (New)
2. Abraham Lincoln : A Complete Biography (New)
3. Mein Kampf : My Struggle (New)
4. Think & Grow Rich (New)
5. The Art of Personality Development (New)
6. Positive Mind Power (New)
7. Travel & Tourism An Industry Facilitator (New)
8. World's Great Authors And Poets (New)
9. Judgment No Aircrash No Death (New)
10. Effective Editing Help Yourself in Becoming A Good Editor (New)
11. Smart House-Keeping for Modern Women
12. Develop Super Power Memory
13. World's Great Personalities
14. Personality Plus
15. Power of Positive Thinking
16. Art of Successful Parenting
17. A Handbook of Etiquettes
18. How to Beat Your Competitors
19. How to Negotiate Effectively
20. World's Great Scientists
21. Patriot The Unique Indian Leader Netaji Subhas Chandra Bose
22. Body Language
23. Art of Successful Living
24. Make Your Boss Happy